£2.50

Afghan Hounds:
A Complete Guide

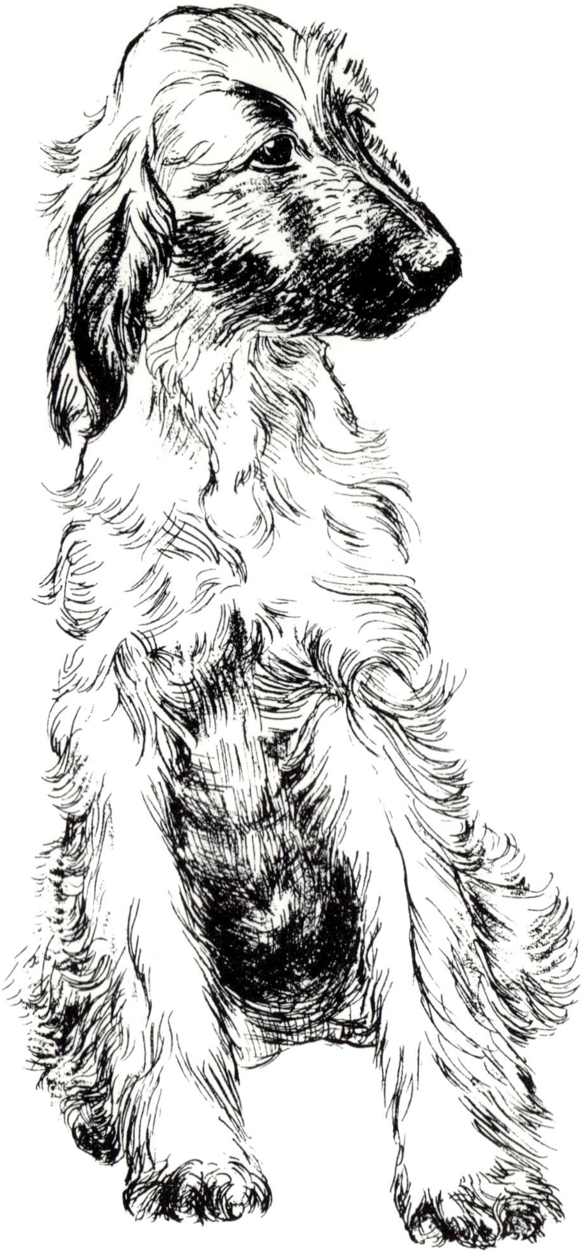

Afghan Hounds:
A Complete Guide

Daphne Gie

David & Charles
Newton Abbot London North Pomfret (Vt) Vancouver

British Library Cataloguing in Publication Data

Gie, Daphne
   Afghan hounds.
   1. Afghan hounds
   I. Title
   636.75'3   SF429.A4

   ISBN 0–7153–7423–0

Library of Congress Catalog Card Number 77-85010

© Daphne Gie 1978

All rights reserved. No part of this
publication may be reproduced, stored
in a retrieval system, or transmitted,
in any form or by any means, electronic,
mechanical, photocopying, recording or
otherwise, without the prior permission
of David & Charles (Publishers) Limited

Printed in Great Britain
by Redwood Burn Limited, Trowbridge & Esher
for David & Charles (Publishers) Limited
Brunel House Newton Abbot Devon

Published in the United States of America
by David & Charles Inc
North Pomfret Vermont 05053 USA

Published in Canada
by Douglas David & Charles Limited
1875 Welch Street North Vancouver BC

To Amber, Kanda, Sahri
and Janus

Contents

	Author's Preface	9
1	Acquiring an Afghan	13
2	Training	30
3	Care and Management	45
4	Sickness and Old Age	59
5	Breeding	74
6	Puppy Rearing	99
7	Showing	109
8	Judging	121
9	Origin and Development	144
10	Breed Clubs and Afghan Standard	175
	Appendix 1 UK Afghan Clubs	199
	Appendix 2 US Afghan Clubs	200
	Bibliography	202
	Acknowledgements	203
	Index	204

Author's Preface

The main reason for the existence of this book is to help all those admirers and possible future owners of Afghans to appreciate the breed to the fullest extent. I have endeavoured to give a comprehensive picture of the life and characteristics of the Afghan, to offer advice on the purchase of a suitable puppy either as a pet or for showing, and also to provide a general idea of the care involved, both in daily life and in breeding the possibilities of showing as a hobby, and all the fascination and interest that can be encountered as a result of a relationship with an Afghan hound.

An Afghan is the most wonderful creature; not only is he remarkably beautiful (when properly cared for), he is also intelligent, independent, loving (though never cloying or sentimental) humourous and a most joyful and entertaining companion. In quick succession he can be a clown, an aloof aristocrat, a lazy, somnolent lounger, suddenly becoming an active, athletic hound ready to tear around the lawn, leap the nearest fence, chase the odd sheep and stay out for hours if the fit so takes him, only to return and hide behind a small blade of grass begging you to have a game of hide and seek.

There is another side to the coin however. His physical attributes and good nature are without question, but he can be disobedient and destructive; he digs frantically and is liable to make complicated earthworks in the most beautiful garden; he can be remarkably deaf when called. He is frequently stubborn and slow at being trained. In fact the screams emitted by a really awkward Afghan during lead training have led to some unfortunate owners being interrogated by the RSPCA. He can also run – very fast!

AUTHOR'S PREFACE

There are unfortunately some misconceptions about the Afghan, one being that he does not need regular grooming as he does not moult. Although he appears in advertisements so frequently with a glossy flowing coat apparently kept in this condition effortlessly and happily, this does not mean that he does not require the attention of a brush and comb; he does – every day. Astonishing though it seems, many people do not realise also how much exercise their pet requires. This is partly due to lack of instruction on the part of the vendor, and also due to the unfortunate publicity gained by the breed in adverts where the dogs are usually shown as the personification of indolence.

One of the worst misunderstandings, and one that is anathema to the serious breeder, is that held by the purchaser who comes along convinced that the Afghan is a rarity of great value, bound to become a champion and able to command the highest price for his services or her progeny. The honest Afghan breeder tries to make it as clear as possible that this fabulous career, for a variety of reasons, may never come to fruition. Unfortunately our words are frequently unheeded.

Connie Miller, a noted American breeder, wrote of the same problem in the USA where the Afghan has suffered a similar population explosion. Quoting from one of her articles in the American publication *Our Afghans* she writes:

> Misconceptions. The Afghan hound is a RARE and VALUABLE dog that with a little bit of luck can become a successful show dog, for any determined owner. Truth. The Afghan is not in the least RARE. In fact, the over-production in this breed (which every breeder blames on all the other breeders) is the breed's number one problem.
>
> Afghans are by far the most difficult of sighthounds to raise, to understand or to place in stable homes – yet remain the most horrendously overproduced breed in the gazehound group. The big demand, in fact about the only REAL demand in this breed is for 'winners'. Every litter of Afghans born is conceived in the name of 'show dog' and stems from a pedigree fat with champions. Practically every Afghan without a disqualifying fault becomes 'show quality'.

Some people buy Afghans because of a wholehearted desire to own one purely as a pet. They love it for its remarkable character,

AUTHOR'S PREFACE

despite its faults, and cope with all the difficulties endemic in owning such a spirited creature. Others buy one because they truly wish to show — they are genuinely interested in the whole procedure, willing to offer their show Afghan a good home and to pay highly to get the best; with luck it will be a contented member of the family whatever the outcome of its career in the ring.

When you have considered very carefully your motive for buying an Afghan and examined all the snags with honesty and realism then you can decide, with genuine regard for this quite remarkable breed, do you really want him for his own sake, or for the reflected glory from his physical beauty and size? Can you supply him with all he needs mentally, physically and emotionally and give him security, freedom and love for the rest of his life, always remembering that he is the 'King of the Dogs'?

Two glamorous champions owned and bred by Mrs Anna Paton. Ch Amudarya Khala in the foreground was Afghan of the year in 1975 and twice Best of Breed at Crufts as well as winning many hound groups and Best In Show awards. Behind is the golden dog, Ch Amudarya the Pagan

AUTHOR'S PREFACE

If you can bear your long awaited puppy,
With constant equanimity and love,
While mopping up the endless round of puddles,
And rescuing the slipper and the glove,
If you can cope with wickedness and cunning,
To make him a cooperative hound,
If you can meet disaster with good humour,
Despite his noise, his chewing teeth, his sound.

If you can groom and not get tired of brushing,
And treat the muddy feet with calm and cool,
If you can face the churned up lawns, wrecked flower beds,
And stop, and put them back with chewed up tool,
If you can hurry back and forth with dishes,
Containing steak and rabbit every day,
Yet not begrudge your hound his daily ration,
Which costs a fortune every time you pay.

If you can win at Crufts and be applauded,
Then show and fail, and not lose heart next day,
If you can take your wins and then your losses,
And feel the judge, and you, have seen fair play,
If you can judge and give your honest verdict,
Nor favour friends nor fear the vicious tongues,
And hear your precious kennel name made mock of,
Your ideals scorned, yet still ignore base wrongs.

If you can nurse a sad and orphaned litter,
Not only day by day but night by night,
And see those tiny puppies fade to nothing,
And still not lose your hopes to win that fight,
If you can fill his life with constant loving,
Provide him with security and care,
Yours is the right to own that glorious Afghan,
His humour, great affection, yours to share.

(Apologies to Rudyard Kipling)

1
Acquiring an Afghan

Most people, wishing to buy an Afghan puppy or even a grown dog, but lacking specialised knowledge and wanting a fairly inexpensive pet, start by looking in the 'Animals for Sale' column of the local paper. This can be a highly frustrating experience, as there may be months between the appearance of local advertisements for Afghans. Also, choice can be limited as a large proportion of these advertisers seem to be one-bitch owners who have had a litter 'for the good of the bitch'. The breeder of the puppies will probably not have wished to spend large sums in travelling a great many miles for a suitable stud dog, or to pay a high stud fee for the services of a champion dog. However, the puppies may very possibly make most beautiful pets and will, in all probability, have been very well reared, for owners who are both proud and fond of a bitch, will undoubtedly do their very best, within reasonable limits, for their offspring. Because the breeder may have limited herself in the choice of a suitable stud dog, the resultant puppies may not be of the highest aesthetic quality, but on the whole the 'one-bitch breeder' need not be approached dubiously: I merely warn you what you may find if what you really want is a 'show dog'. The next obvious source for the would-be owner is the 'Yellow Pages' of the telephone directory, and a search through the dog-breeders and boarding-kennel section usually produces adverts for Afghans. Here may be found the large kennels, often dealing with the production of several breeds as well as boarding, and most willing and able to produce several litters a year; also, if they have not got what you want, they are bound to know – via the infallible doggy grapevine – someone who has.

These larger kennels who, because they run as a business, find it to their advantage to pay quite a high fee to advertise in the 'Yellow Pages', often show their dogs and have a considerable range in the lines of their bitches and stud dogs. They are also willing to travel widely to use the type of stud dog they consider most suitable for their bitch, and may consequently produce a happier blending of types. Of equal importance is the fact that such kennels have a reputation to uphold both for breeding and rearing, although even then the buyer may have the misfortune to contact a shyster. I must here add one word of warning – frequently there appear advertisements in the papers from enormous kennel concerns or animal supermarkets. You name the breed and they stock it, or, if not, they will get it. These are not the places at which to buy your Afghan. Often the puppy comes from some 'get rich quick' merchant who breeds frequently, rears cheaply and sells at relatively low prices for a quick profit: even some of the pedigrees supplied are suspect. All too often the puppies are poor and ailing and can only be a source of perpetual disappointment. As many of these kennels buy at short notice and sometimes, even by telephone, they take in good faith what is offered for quick turnover, and, as they do not have facilities for checking pedigrees, there can be no comeback when some puppy, acquired with enormous expectations, turns out to be a complete failure. To quote an oft-seen car sticker, 'Buy from a Breeder'.

If a prospective owner cares to ring the Kennel Club, he will be given a list of Afghan breeders in his area and also the name of the area Afghan club secretary, who will be only too willing to advise on buying a puppy. From these sources the prospective purchaser will be given not only some of the addresses that he found in the 'Yellow Pages', but also the names of Afghan enthusiasts who do not run a huge boarding establishment or dog business and therefore do not advertise so widely or expensively, but who may own, as a hobby bordering on a small business, anything from ten to thirty Afghans. As breeders and quite often experienced judges, they will rear their litters well, having the interest of the breed at heart, and be able to advise on relevant points when a client needs assistance. The purchaser should also buy the advantages of a complete 'after sales' service from a reputable breeder. For this breed, which looks so deceptively simple in youth, with its soft short coat and the sleek straight hair so frequently pictured in maturity, breeder–buyer contact is essential as even the most sincere and earnest owner can come to grief with a coat that has picked up little twigs and burrs and becomes hopelessly tangled in the process. Every genuine Afghan breeder will happily invite clients back in order that they can see how the dog they sold has progressed and, as the coat grows, will if necessary give a complete groom as an example of the correct method. Similarly, they should be prepared to answer the endless questions on health, behaviour and diet, with which they can be bombarded patiently: after all, this is a breed with a most tricky sense of humour which loves frightening its parents to distraction by refusing food or limping for no apparent reason – this latter little trick only becomes obvious when the wretched creature happens to forget which paw it was favouring and limps on the other side. However, may I here put in a plea on behalf of the breeder's welfare since I forget how many times I have been 'phoned in the early hours of the morning by an anxious owner about some triviality which could well have waited until later.

Another argument in favour of dedicated breeders is the fact that they usually have plenty of space to house both young stock and adults and are therefore able to have a puppy inoculated and quarantined for the required period, should the purchaser so desire. This is convenient to a new owner, especially when the puppy is going to live in a thickly populated area where there may be more risk of infection from other dogs. They will also have seen that the puppies are properly wormed and in excellent health before being offered for sale.

A most obvious source of information as to the whereabouts of puppies is the 'For Sale' columns of the two journals, *Dog World* and *Our Dogs,* published at the end of each week. Here can be found adverts from breeders great and small all over the British Isles. A great many have a tendency to make out that their geese are swans, but if you want only a pet, every one of them will have some delightful little personage tucked away in the litter, who has, perhaps, a slightly rounder eye or a straighter shoulder than would befit a champion, but carries superb breeding and a lovely temperament. Only a judge would know the difference between this one and the pick of the litter and your puppy would, in all probability, have many famous dogs in his pedigree. These papers, as an added extra, contain many articles on dog matters, which will interest the most uninformed novice and, although not written with Afghans specifically in mind, contain much sound wisdom, garnered over many years of varied experience in dogdom, which is, indeed, a world of its own. They will also help to stabilise and bring just a little closer to earth, the idealistic, head-in-the-clouds admirer of beautiful dogs by their salty humour and extremely basic facts.

The actual purchase of your puppy, often so long awaited, is truly an exciting experience. Try therefore to approach the business of choosing your small hound with a modicum of common sense, cold detachment and firm control over your own very natural enthusiasm. Do your utmost not to be too carried away at the sight of several small, lively puppies all vying with each other for your attention to use your critical faculties. Instead, consciously use your eyes, ears and nose. Look first at the general condition of the litter – are they relatively clean? It is, of course, necessary to qualify that term since healthy, active puppies can always find something to satisfy their mischievous and destructive urges, even overturning their water bowl and wallowing in the ensuing mud, or scratching and rolling in any soft earth. A little local grubbiness can be appreciated and forgiven but sticky, felted coats with dirt engrained to the skin are not acceptable. Runs should be reasonably clean, although obviously all puppies foul them occasionally, but there should not be a horrid accumulation of turds nor any sign of diarrhoea. Well fed puppies which have been properly wormed should have firm motions.

Your nose will soon tell you if the pups have been kept in clean kennels with a regular change of bedding. There should be no sad whining or whimpering – healthy, boisterous Afghans have loud, challenging barks from an early age. Notice also whether eyes are clear and bright or is there a tendency for them to be runny, sticky or have puffy lids? At some time during your inspection look to see if there is any sign of pink haws, an enlargement of the third eyelid at the inner corner of the eye, which is pink or white instead of dark like the eyelid. This is considered a fault in British Afghans, although not specifically mentioned in the breed standard. In America it is not considered so harshly, as I discovered when I mentioned my dislike of it and the fact that it affected my judgement of some singularly beautiful dogs. Whatever the various opinions, my own feeling is that it ruins that clear, aloof, steady gaze normally expected from the adult Afghan, particularly one with a very dark mask and eye.

Consider most carefully the general condition of the whole litter, not just your chosen puppy. Look for strength, muscle, firm bodies and the lean but sturdy loins apparent even in a ten week old. The straight strong bones of the forelegs should have no sign of weakness and the young coat should have a gloss on it. If the puppies have obviously weak, bent bones, swollen joints, very bad pot bellies, running noses, sore spots on their tummies, or are not clean, excuse yourself politely and go elsewhere.

Age is a prime consideration when buying a puppy; do not be conned into purchasing some excessively immature little chap because you feel sorry for it. If it starts off as difficult to leave for a few hours and a terrible problem to feed, you are going to become disenchanted very soon, and your first few weeks together will be a disaster, not a pleasure. Some breeders are known to sell their puppies at five weeks which is dreadfully young for what is literally a baby, to leave its siblings and become a solitary entity. True, it may be fully capable of eating well and scampering around, but it still needs to cuddle up to something warm and comforting. Undoubtedly, there are some who may be better off sold to an understanding owner rather than living with the breeder who cares only for its possible monetary value. Nevertheless, the puppy could fall into the hands of someone who does not understand its needs.

Some years ago, the Afghan Hound Association drew up a code of ethics for breeders, to which all their members were expected to adhere. This was excellent, because it brought the criteria for well reared, well bred puppies into the open. Amongst other things it urged that puppies should be kept until at least two months of age, and that they should be sold inoculated and wormed and, to this end, they issue a most informative leaflet. However, it seems all right to sell large, strong puppies from eight weeks onwards; by then, they have definite little personalities and are capable of exerting themselves, expressing their wants and feelings and well able to start a new life. In these days of cash shortage, it may be better for

ACQUIRING AN AFGHAN

breeders to maintain their puppies really well for eight weeks, then sell, rather than to be unable to meet, adequately, the demands of rapidly increasing appetites.

If the breeder is comparatively inexperienced and has not asked someone with wider knowledge to help sort out the litter for show and pet quality, then you may be offered the whole litter from which to choose yours. In that case, it is easier to make a preliminary choice of a few that really appeal to you, then ask the breeder to put the others out of sight. Having thus narrowed down the choice, you can more easily concentrate on choosing 'the one', often a very difficult matter. Disregard the ones that won't come

Puppies at three weeks old bear little resemblance to the finished object with their short smooth coats, although the knobbly occiput is already becoming obvious (*Chris Hill*)

near you, are shy or unwilling to know people; look instead for the puppy that really has a major interest in you, for they seem to have a sixth sense which tells them that someone is making a decision which will affect the whole of their life. Remember that the whole relationship is going to be a long interchange of feelings and experience between the two of you and therefore it is useless, and to a large extent cruel, to take one that has not willingly chosen you and who does not find you at all an attractive person.

We make a great feature of making would-be purchasers realise that their Afghan must approve of them and come to them of its own volition before we will let them have it. I have no doubt that we regularly insult people who feel that they should be put before the dogs, but usually find that we ensure our puppies a permanent and stable home. I have also quite ruthlessly turned people away who have seemed unsuitable in their attitude, or unable or unwilling to provide the proper accommodation, adequate attention and sufficient arrangements for exercise.

If you genuinely desire to show your Afghan and make him a hobby as well as a pet, you will certainly need to have more knowledge when making your choice. The breeder, if experienced, will undoubtedly wish to help and advise you, therefore you will probably be shown only the best in the litter. Be honest however, do not keep your intentions a close secret; you may be charged a few pounds more for the best in the litter, but it is better for both parties concerned, because if you buy only a pet Afghan, you will undoubtedly suffer considerable and possibly frequent and hurtful disappointment when your pride and joy doesn't win. Equally, it will be a mortifying experience for the breeder to see a dog with his or her prefix consistently eliminated from the winning line up, or – to quote an unfortunate dog show colloquialism – 'thrown out with the rubbish'.

It is an excellent idea to thoroughly digest the Kennel Club standard of the breed before selecting your puppy in order to gain an idea of all the points for which you should be looking. Subsequently, you should be able to visualise the general proportion of the animal and details such as the shape of the eyes, the feet and the type of head. There is of course a difficulty in that the standard describes an adult dog in full coat, but nevertheless, if you are considering a puppy that will eventually be shown, it is necessary to look carefully at the conformation of the puppy with relation to the standard. It is obviously easier to choose such a puppy at three months rather than eight weeks, since there is more bone growth and maturity and it is also somewhat easier to look for a 'balanced' youngster. Most serious breeders, if intending that some of the litter are for sale as show dogs, keep these pups on for a few weeks longer than ones that will be sold purely as pets.

At this age, the puppy will still be somewhat ungainly and unglamorous though nevertheless attractive and full of charm. He will have a short but slightly tufty coat with definite saddle markings down the back. His head carriage should already be high and proud and his movement firm and steady with a definite tendency towards a 'style of high order'.

If at this stage he is narrow either in front or behind; if he is cow-hocked (hocks tending to turn in towards each other, particularly during movement), he will not grow into a really sound hound, since at this age there should be a greater comparative width between both fore- and hindlegs than at any other period of his development. On the contrary, the dog narrow at the sternum will become one who may look magnificent when seen moving from the side, but appear to have 'two pins out of one hole' when viewed from the front.

Seen from the side, a dog or bitch should ideally be almost square with the same length from chest to the base of the tail as from the top of the shoulder to the ground. In movement, he should have a firm, thrusting stride which does not cause a great upheaval along the puppy's back (sometimes, dogs appear to have an almost caterpillar, looping action along the topline during movement) and his hindfeet should never touch or extend beyond his forefeet when moving at an extended gait.

The head of the youngster will still be immature, but do not necessarily fall for the finest and narrowest, since this type could become overfine as the dog grows, and, in fact, may turn out to be shorter in the muzzle than the one who has a little more width at the end of the nose. I am not by any means advocating that you should choose a coarse head, but do remember that a fully grown Afghan should have a punishing jaw and sufficient breadth of skull to ensure a sound brain and the intelligence that goes with a hunting dog. The Afghan does not have a collie head.

The skull will be long rather than broad but will basically have a fairly wide, oval shape, ending in a prominent knob at the back; this knob is called the occiput and a really good occipital bone indicates that there will be reasonable growth in the length of the head.

The foreface from the 'stop' (slight indentation of the nasal bone which occurs just between the eyes) will finally balance in length with the skull, but at this age, the foreface will probably be slightly shorter. There should, however, be definite indications of a 'Roman nose' with a slight but definite bump just before the end. On no account should you choose one with a rather depressed nasal bone as it will almost certainly turn out to have a 'dish face' without the true, haughty expression of an Afghan.

Eyes should not be too full or round but should have a definite triangular shape. Nevertheless, because of the problems caused by a tiny eye in too fine a skull, there is evidence that eye troubles of varying types can form later if the eyeball is too small. The bone under the eye should be delicately modelled and not too wide, or you may find a broad foreface developing. Note also that the ears commence level with the outer corner of the eye – too high an ear set will ruin the general shape of the dog's head in later life.

Check that the dentition of the puppy is complete and that the puppy has a scissor bite, or somewhat rarely, a level bite. If the teeth are slightly overshot there is no cause for alarm since it will most probably even out as the puppy grows; however, an undershot or wry mouth will remain forever and will be faulted in the ring.

The furry fuzz or 'monkey whiskers' which form on many puppy faces is perfectly correct and accepted in the breed, even though some youngsters do not acquire them. Many breeders claim that puppies with these quite adorable whiskers eventually have heavier coats, but I have found no actual proof of this in my own breeding.

Ch Badakshan Rani, owned by Mr and Mrs Ronald Adams, photographed as a nine-week-old puppy and then as a titled adult. These pictures show the development of a self-possessed puppy into an elegant, balanced bitch. The shoulder and hind angulation can be seen clearly and the general conformation can be assessed with an eye to future growth

Although the proportion of the growing youngster can change considerably as a result of an uneven growth pattern, beware of the puppy whose head seems perilously close to its shoulders. In an adult, an equal length from nose to occiput and from occiput to base of neck is a fairly good guide. Consequently, the puppy should show signs that this proportion will develop, as also will an inclination to a slightly 'horsey' arch in the neck.

Shoulder angulation of the puppy will be visible as will the angle and proportion of the upper arm, and the shoulder blade should be at an angle of 45° to the ground. This is being somewhat idealistic however, and one can really only say to the novice, 'Don't choose a puppy where the placement of the shoulder blade continues upward so that there is a nearly straight line from the forearm.' Since this is probably one of the most difficult features to assess, it is wise to trust the guidance of the breeder, or any experienced friend who agrees to help you.

When choosing your show puppy, take care to avoid selecting one with too long a body or a 'dippy' back. The proportion from the sternum to the end of the rib cage should be longer than that from the end of the rib, along the loin to the pelvis but as the rib contains the 'works' of the heart and lung, it goes without saying that an athletic dog needs plenty of room for both heart and lungs without too much 'barrelling' out sideways, and a short muscular loin.

An Afghan's hip bones must be fairly prominent even in a pleasingly plump puppy, and though he may be a little high on the rump until his quarters 'let down' completely with maturity, it should be quite obvious exactly where his tail set occurs in relation to the hip bones and the 'fallaway' or croup. If it is set very near the hip bones, then the tail will always be too high set and will either flop over the back or be carried too gaily. It should be remembered that the tail is an extension of the back bone and is set fairly low, though not held between the legs when standing, nor must it dangle like a piece of limp string. It is raised in movement and even as a puppy this shows quite clearly, as also the fact that the tail will be starting to ring in the characteristic doughnut fashion. The croup will gradually acquire more of a slope as the youngster grows and the quarters mature and let down.

Fore- and hindlegs must be well boned and the joints at this stage should be large and extremely pronounced. The feet should be large with the forefeet rather broader so that the puppy's legs seem ungainly and heavy as you look down the straight, comparatively slender bones of the forelegs to the increasing size of the joint and finally to the huge feet. However, all this evens out beautifully as the puppy grows, and the large long feet are an indication of his future size. Whatever happens, provided that you are sure that your puppy is in excellent condition, do not allow yourself to be dismayed by the 'know alls' with little specialised information, who will undoubtedly, on seeing your puppy's knobbly joints, exclaim with horror, 'That pups got rickets, you've been done' – you haven't.

The hindlegs should show signs of their future angulation, unless you are buying when he is six months old or more; as the puppy grows, the hindlegs tend to become straighter for some time, and the rear end tends to become higher than its back. This is purely temporary however, and the angulation will reappear with more maturity, and as the whole rear assembly takes its final position.

There should be a promise of good length to the upper and lower thigh from the hip to the hock, and the length from the hock to the hindfoot should be proportionately shorter. However, beware of the over angulation so beloved by many of today's judges who applaud glamour before the essence of the hunting hound, and which is gradually ruining the strength of the hindquarters. Too open an angle from the hip bone to the femur spells weakness.

Watch the puppy you fancy both as it moves and standing. Already the carriage will be firm and proud, but also check that the angle of its feet in both circumstances are level and straight. They should not turn or be thrown inward or outward in movement, nor should there be any awkward movement from any leg.

However, try to remember, while not getting too confused over all the points that you wish to note, that the Afghan has, in its native country, always been bred as a hunting hound and should still bear those characteristics.

Do not be misled by any statements regarding colour and its value: our standard states very clearly that all colours are acceptable. One hears of fantastic prices being charged for colours that used to be a rarity such as the delicate blues or showy brindles. However, as we feel more and more the influence of imported American stock with its very wide colour range, these price anomalies will doubtless fade. Basically, it is the structure of the dog underneath the coat that is all important and the colour is virtually the painting that completes the picture. Just go ahead, choose the dog which you most admire and wish to own, regardless of whether it is black, white or multicoloured. Once chosen, check that your puppy has been adequately wormed and you will also require a diet sheet to ensure continuity in the puppy's feeding, so that there is not a complete and unsettling change for the puppy or a lack of necessary supplements such as calcium because of the purchaser's insufficient knowledge. It is possible that the breeder will be able to arrange insurance for both value and third party. The Dog Breeders' Insurance Company is a popular and reliable firm who will insure your puppy for value as well as issuing an excellent third-party cover for a suitable extra charge. The National Dog Owners' Association, a very worthwhile institution with the interests of dog owners at heart also arrange a comprehensive insurance which provides benefits for owners who have to board their dogs through hospitalisation. It ill behoves anyone with any breed of dog, particularly an Afghan, to be without third-party cover, since any large dog is fair game for accusations of damage: legislation now puts the onus for damage fairly and squarely on the owner and indeed, in the event of any dog getting loose, tearing across the road and causing an accident which results in damage running into many thousands of pounds, the owner is liable for considerable costs.

You should receive your puppy's pedigree for an outright payment although in the event of terms such as a 'loan of bitch' agreement (with the co-operation of the Kennel Club), where you arrange to give payment in the form of puppies, at a later date, you may not receive the official pedigree until the terms of the contract

Ch Khanabad White Warrior bred and owned by Miss Margaret Niblock. A most spectacular white dog, proving that the colour of a dog is immaterial and that there is no need for it to be black masked to win. In fact a self-coloured mask can be most expressive

are fulfilled. If the pedigree is not forthcoming when you have paid the full price of the puppy, query the fact: you can encounter some very odd deals. Do not be put off by some tale that the breeder will send it later – they must have all details of the stock used. If you decide to buy your puppy on hire purchase or some form of breeding terms, make sure that you have a written contract of which both you and the breeder have a signed copy. Registrations are occasionally delayed, if the owner has, for example, been uncertain of the colours his dark little puppies may develop, therefore the registration card and the Kennel Club transfer form from breeder to purchaser may have to be sent later. However, do check carefully, particularly if you intend to show or breed, that the puppy is correctly registered with the Kennel Club, otherwise, however beautiful the dog or excellent its pedigree, it can never be shown or used for breeding. If the breeder does not register your puppy, you are perfectly at liberty to do so, provided that you have the full names and registration numbers of both the parents. This is now a generally accepted procedure since the introduction of the basic registration and the active registration, the Kennel Club's new two-tier system. Here the breeder registers basically the number of bitches and dogs in a litter within one month of their birth. They are then given a breeder's pack of registration forms which they can either take up themselves, thus giving each puppy their kennel name, or give the appropriate form to the new owner to register the puppy if and when they please. However, once the puppy is purchased, the new owner can show him or her, if they wish—unless the registration card has been endorsed (at the Kennel Club) 'not for exhibition' or 'not to be bred from'.

I shall never forget in the days before these endorsements became possible selling a pet bitch to a gentleman who attempted to argue me down to an abnormally low price, by pointing to all the children he flourished in front of me, swearing that he certainly did not ever intend to show, but desperately wanted a pet. I produced a charming youngster with unfortunate large round eyes like car lamps, and to my mind, rather straight stifles. He returned a week later with the money to collect her, and no sooner had he received his signed transfer form when he asked 'How do I go about showing her?' In vain I argued that he assured me that he wanted only a pet, and that was what she was. I did not want her shown. She appeared in the ring many times and did quite well, even at championship shows. However, when he finally asked the world at large at a crowded benching tent at one of our large summer championship shows why his dog could never make the grade to become a champion, I found enormous satisfaction in saying equally loudly 'Because you asked for and received a pet.'

Most breeders are fully willing to give a novice owner advice on grooming and are equally willing to give a complete after-sales service answering questions on behaviour, training, health and coat care. The breeder has a definite responsibility to both purchaser and puppy for their future happiness and well-being together. I always encourage my clients to bring back their puppies regularly, where this is possible, and to offer any necessary help. It is of enormous interest to see how various compoundings of breeding develop. No one however, can guarantee perfection, and in all honesty, one can say only that the little puppy has no visible defects and, as it stands at the time of purchase, is of good quality and shows promise. One cannot make a firm undertaking that any living creature will fulfil that early promise, and certainly no one can quite specifically state that it will become a champion.

Once having bought your puppy, take it home, forget all the others in the litter that you saw, and don't allow second thoughts to encroach about the other one you nearly chose — did we really pick the best? Settle down to enjoy the latest addition to the family and remember too that, whatever your hopes and ambitions in the Afghan world may be, first and foremost your Afghan should be your companion and devoted friend; a show dog and a future champion is very much a secondary attraction.

2
Training

Every Afghan needs training. No matter how excellent his pedigree, how charming and obliging his nature, how well behaved his parents were, he will need patient and careful guidance if he is to be a pleasant, acceptable member of the household, and a joy to take visiting rather than a total embarrassment. That is one of the reasons breeders are so wary of selling to households where everyone that can be considered responsible to the puppy goes out to work. It is also a reason why so many Afghans brought up in such circumstances find themselves thrust upon rescue schemes and even on occasions are put to sleep.

From the moment a puppy enters his new home, his social and 'house training' begin. First of all pop him straight out into his future place of exercise (which, hopefully, will be as near the door as possible), in order to relieve himself after his journey. On the one hand, cheerful words of praise and encouragement as soon as he performs will make him realise that he is pleasing you and this will give him a good start in meeting his new family. On the other, his first moments in a new home should not be marred by a mad rush to mop up the puddle that he has unwittingly made on the carpet, while he stands alone and bewildered.

As soon as he appears to need to relieve himself again, he should be taken to the same place, through the same door, in the same direction. During the intervals when he is left during the night, for as long as he is too young to contain himself entirely, a thick wad of newspaper should be placed in front of the door out of which he is taken. It is then a simple matter, if he starts to make a puddle in the middle of the kitchen floor, to whisk him onto the paper with an appropriate word. The newspaper on the floor will be needed for only a limited period, since, once he is sufficiently mature to wait until you let him out first thing in the morning he will then dash straight out to his own 'patch'. If some short, easily learnt phrase, such as 'quickly now' or 'spend pennies', is used on each occasion he will soon associate it with the action and should then oblige fairly easily. It is also a great advantage if he performs to a magic word when you are staying at a hotel and want no mistakes.

Your small Afghan must be put outside immediately after each meal and you should at first keep an eye on him in order to make sure that he has done all that is necessary before allowing him inside again, meanwhile murmuring your magic formula. Do remember to give plenty of praise when he does oblige so that he realises that he has done the correct thing, and he can see the reason for being put outside in the first place.

Although it may seem a tedious chore it really is necessary to keep popping him outside at quite frequent intervals during the day, since he has only a small bladder and in his little mind he will be trying desperately hard not to displease you. Make him realise, however, it is not just playtime but there is a purpose involved.

If he does make a mistake point it out to him, firmly but quietly. Shouting leads only to bewilderment and is not a sensible part of any training. Show him what he has done while it is still fresh in his mind then say whatever words of disapproval you are going to use. Once more make it short and easily remembered such as 'No, naughty.' Then show him the way outside with the appropriate word. You must make sure, however, that the dog realises just why you are saying all these things, therefore your tone can be exaggerated. Training an Afghan certainly gives good practice in histrionics!

It should not be necessary to spank your Afghan if you speak gently and firmly in a strong, quiet voice. This gives him confidence and understanding. Occasionally one finds a remarkably stubborn one who delights in disobedience and here a quick slap on his behind (but never on his bony hip joints) will soon teach him the error of his ways if accompanied by a reproachful and indignant voice. Equally a very light tap on the nasal bone with a folded newspaper does not hurt in the least but the sound in the nasal cavity causes him to pause and think.

On no account should you ever be violent. He will become stubborn and maladjusted or cowed – a truly dreadful sight.

At no time should any dog be allowed to foul the pavement and public footpaths. This has always been an unsavoury aspect of the pet dog with the anti-social owner, and it ill behoves any of us to allow this to happen with such a noticeable dog, particularly in these days of the anti-dog campaigns and the perpetual threats of parliamentary bills to increase licence fees to astronomical proportions. It is alarming at times to see the messes allowed to accumulate outside dog shows by uncaring owners. Everyone should be aware of the fines that can be imposed by town and borough councils for such behaviour. From the start, train your dog to use the gutter or some patch of waste land where he cannot be accused of nuisance. As soon as you see him start to squat put him quickly in the gutter, keeping him firmly under control. Until he has relieved himself on an outing he should walk near the edge of the pavement where he can be moved in time. I am, of course, assuming that the owner is sufficiently sensible not to dash off the pavement into the traffic. When your dog is, at command, using the gutter, carefully position yourself between him and the oncoming traffic. Do not, as I have seen owners do, stand away at the far end of the lead, disclaiming all responsibility for your dog, who is, after all, only exercising a perfectly natural function. He is at risk.

In all respects his life should begin as you intend it to continue. Choose a convenient, quiet corner of the kitchen where he can always eat quietly without being disturbed. There he should have his first meal and there he will always find his bowl of clean fresh water. The word 'dinner' frequently repeated will quickly be recognised. If his sleeping quarters are in the same corner all the better. That is his secure 'home'.

When he first arrives in your home, the new puppy will have been used to feeding with the rest of the litter: this means that he would always have had to eat quickly in order to get his share. Therefore at first he will still probably eat quite quickly. Conversely he may be nonplussed by the quiet feeding conditions. However, if you continue quietly about your business while he is eating, he will soon adapt to the different conditions and eat like any other dog. Whatever happens, if he is a tardy eater try to avoid giving him his food in little pieces from your fingers. He will quickly seize upon this as a means of getting attention, and at the same time he will have established mental ascendancy over you. As a result he will, if necessary, go to dire extremes, sometimes almost starving himself to death in order to gain that extra hold over his owner. On one occasion I sold a fat, lively puppy to a lady who tearfully brought it back about six weeks later, literally a handful of skin and bone. She assured me that it refused all food although she would get on her knees and beg it to eat, sometimes weeping over it. After she departed I cooked a cheese omelette for it with a fried onion filling, (both flavours very dear to the Afghan heart and stomach) popped the puppy into a kennel, looked him in the eye and said firmly 'eat it'. Puppy looked at me as I closed the door with what can only be described as a twinkle in his eye, and within minutes the omelette was consumed. I have always been convinced that this very strong-minded little fellow would have killed himself, just for the sheer pleasure of seeing that poor woman on her knees before him, knowing that he had mastered her.

Do not be tempted to feed titbits from the table and do not allow guests to do so either. No one wants a massive hairy paw thrust into their pâté, nor a long nose lurking near their soup, nor do they wish to find that their steak has been adroitly abstracted from the left while they have been in conversation with their neighbour on the right. Not only do you not want a nuisance who will alienate all your friends but it is bad for your dog to be overindulged.

Somehow, whatever his age, an Afghan's nose is always at the correct height to whisk the most tempting morsel from the table. At first he will surreptitiously stand on the opposite side of the table (hopefully unseen) and lever himself up by his paws. This is easily detected by the fact that he pushes things around in the process. As he grows he reverts from the elegant Eastern gentleman to the cunning Pathani thief, and is able to take a joint of meat in his jaws with no apparent trace as he passes by. The only way to stop him is by a firm 'No' and a slap on the rump or the use of a folded newspaper – right from the start. It is useless to stand and laugh indulgently at the puppy antics, then worry because he turns into an incorrigible thief. It is also a good idea to keep all the doors closed.

An interesting fact to consider is that a dog who decides not to eat for no valid reason, though in the best of health, may well decide to eat if his food is put into a different dish and placed on a table ostensibly out of reach and he is left in a situation where he can 'steal' it.

Do not allow your puppy to carry his food about all over the house and quietly hoard it in odd corners for future reference. Afghans are prone to hiding little extras in odd corners all over the place. I once found a most carefully folded paper parcel under a chair in my sitting room where a dog had actually wrapped his half-empty food bowl in a piece of newspaper – and a very neat job he had made of it too. Their long noses are most useful when it comes to burying things outside, inside chairs, or behind cupboards and they can often be heard pushing away at things with a strange squeak like a slate pencil caused by the leathery nose rubbing over a hard surface.

TRAINING

Train him from the very beginning to sleep in his own bed. However difficult and exhausting this may be for the first night or so the effort will be well worth the result. If he is tucked up firmly with a soft, chewy, cuddly toy (a large sock stuffed with stockings is ideal) a hot-water bottle under his blanket to simulate the warmth of all the other little bodies he has been used to, if it is cold weather, and a loud ticking clock to break the silence and keep him company, then he should be perfectly peaceful throughout the night. Make sure that his bed is in a warm place, however, so that he is not disturbed by a piercing draught. If his howls are too loud and you have to come down to him to try to settle him down in his own bed, try to discover what caused him to be disturbed in the first place. If you take him up to bed with you then you will have created a precedent and for him this is the thin edge of the wedge; he will merely have exchanged one set of bedfellows for a larger species.

There is no hard-and-fast rule about what settles a puppy during the first night alone; sometimes a warm drink helps, but if neighbours are very near then you can administer a very tiny sedative to make him drowsy enough to forget his troubles and go to sleep. Even sleeping is to a certain extent a matter of training and habit. No sedative or tranquilliser should ever be administered to an Afghan except on veterinary advice.

A young Afghan with his jaw full of large developing teeth is also an inveterate chewer. He chewed at the rest of the litter before he came to you and he will continue in the same manner unless firmly restrained.

I think that this use of the jaw is a basic Pathani trait since at one period in the 1870s the Afghanistan postal system required that corners of stamps be bitten off by the postman in order to cancel them. Puppies of this breed treat carpet corners, furniture, shoes, or anything the right size in exactly the same way. The easiest way to avoid such troubles is to resolve never to give your puppy an old slipper or shoe to chew. It is asking too much to expect him to differentiate between his own slipper and yours. Give him a bone or his own toys in his own patch where he can be as destructive as he pleases. When he is indoors make it very plain that certain things are taboo. He will understand after constant repetition, particularly if he has been sufficiently exercised so that he has not too much surplus energy to get rid of indoors.

Some Afghans are quicker to learn than others and allowances must be made for the slow learners. There are also dogs which are unusually sensitive and their feelings get desperately hurt when they make a mistake. Whatever your reactions may be to some peccadillo on their part, do not be tempted to overscold for these can be hurt out of all proportion to the crime, while the bolder ones can almost be heard taking the attitude 'She's off again.' Constant but gentle repetition is the thing.

Make sure right from the beginning that he knows his name. That is his claim to individuality and being, and if you frequently use it he begins to feel real and identified. Always use his name when training him – 'Pasha sit', and 'Pasha heel' – and he will soon realise that these instructions apply to him. He will soon learn from the tone of your voice what you require in the way of behaviour.

Introduce him carefully and systematically to all who come to the house. You do not want to be saddled with a shy dog who is terrified to meet people, or a suspicious creature who guards the home against everyone.

Although you will naturally wish to show off your charmer of a puppy, and every visitor will wish to play with him, be vigilant not to let him become overexcited and boisterous. It is at this stage that they can bounce too high, tear cushions in their play, rip at clothes, lacerate hands with their sharp little teeth and leave little damp trails on the carpet. When this happens, pop him quickly outside to cool down with a word of encouragement so that he knows that he really isn't in disgrace. He will soon learn to behave beautifully and quietly for short periods if treated sensibly and, as he grows and his powers of concentration increase, so, for longer periods, he will be perfectly behaved company.

All house training is really a matter of common sense, and temptations should, as far as possible, be kept out of your Afghan's way, by keeping things shut away and all doors closed. To prevent him from being a nuisance, control must be established in order to stop him from galloping all over without ceasing. He must therefore be made to sit and lie down at your command.

To train him to sit down, say 'sit' firmly, at the same time holding him firmly under his breast bone with one hand and pressing on his rear to the ground with the other. As he gets up repeat the action and word again and then gently holding him there say 'stay' in the same tone. This must be repeated several times at intervals and progress will not necessarily be rapid. Indeed most Afghans are too interested in the world about them to allow small matters such as training to worry them unduly. A little titbit for trying often helps and Afghans are quick to learn that co-operation brings its own rewards. I emphasise *co-operation*; not *submission*. A small piece of mousetrap cheese or a morsel of fried sausage or fried liver work wonders and when I am training a dog I always have polythene bags of such tempters in my pocket.

To make him lie down repeat the process, but once the dog is in the sitting position one can press on the shoulders. This makes some dogs lie down automatically. Or, while holding the dog in a sitting position, pull the front legs forward (not too hastily) and he will automatically lie down. Once more use the command that you intend to use permanently and make him lie there for a minute or two at a time until he comes to realise that this is a moment when he is supposed to be at rest.

I feel that I must emphasise again that some Afghans take more time to train than others. This I imagine is where the idea comes from that they are completely untrainable. Some are more intelligent than others and some, like humans, are exceedingly bashful and selfconscious and hesitate to try in case they do it all wrong.

The same method of training is used to teach your dog to lie down for his grooming, or to stand, in whichever way you intend to carry out this operation. Training right from the day you acquire your puppy will save a great deal of frustration and anger for you and a great deal of misery for the dog.

Lead training should also be undertaken at the earliest possible moment but the puppy should not be taken anywhere near a road until you have him firmly and happily under control and he understands what is required of him, while having complete confidence in the handler.

TRAINING

First put a light collar on his neck, but not too tightly. I let mine wear their collars for a couple of days (taking them off at night), until it is such a part of their general life that they do not even think about it.

Routine can have strange results. We once at Christmas, for example, put a very old Honourable Artillery Company tie round the neck of one of my special pets as he ate his dinner. After that he insisted on having it on at each meal and no other tie would do. This went on for ages, with the tie constantly being washed and becoming more and more threadbare until no regiment would have owned it.

The next stage is to attach the lead — a light leather one not a heavy jangly object which can frighten the dog. Do not make the mistake of trying to force an independent spirited youngster to walk where you want to go immediately; instead walk with him so that he realises that you are attached but are not impeding him. Have a savoury titbit handy and keep it hidden in the lead hand nearest to him, holding the lead's loop in your right hand with the length passed across in front of you to be held in the left hand with the puppy on your left side. He will smell the sausage and, lifting his nose, walk with you in the direction you want. Take a few turns up and down the garden this way, giving him a tasty morsel at intervals and talking to him to maintain his interest. Make sure he learns the command 'Heel!' as you walk along and keep encouraging him in a cheerful, loving voice.

Two or three minutes of this at a time is quite sufficient for a first experience with a lead. Repeat it two or three times daily, making him sit beside you at command to have his lead attached and then starting off with the word 'heel', on the left foot. Use his name frequently so that he is in no doubt about your intentions. Make this part of his training so pleasant that he will really enjoy learning and he will then be eager to accompany you on any excursion.

Afghans are like children, eager to learn and anxious to be busy about something, and if this involves their owner what could be better? However, like children they are better at co-operating than being blindly obedient, so on no account pull at his lead to make him do what you want when he is inexperienced and undecided.

Ch Wazir of Desertaire and English Ch Waliwog of Carloway enjoying the snow with their owner Sheila Devitt. Wazir was destined to hand down colour and showmanship and 'Wiggy' to sire some beautiful stock, most notably the goldens Ch Ranjitsinhji and Ch Rasta of Jagai, before going to the Fermoy kennel of David Roche in Australia

This will merely frighten him and cause him to fight and scream while you will find yourself dragging a recalcitrant pup along behind you on its back.

As soon as he walks sensibly with you and understands the word 'heel', commence teaching him to sit and stay close beside you so that you can safely pause at the kerb without the risk of his dashing off in front of you to the length of his lead. Even that could cause pain and death. Since sitting and staying are part of his social training, pause in your walk, press his rear end down and say firmly, 'Sit and stay!'

Once he is sufficiently used to your routine to trust you implicitly, in spite of strange noises, the time has come to take him out into the larger world outside. Do not immediately plunge him into the centre of a busy town. Take him first into a quiet road where he can learn to walk steadily along the pavements and not dash to either side when a noisy vehicle approaches, and not to jump up on passing strangers. This is the time to train him to use the gutter if the necessity arises. Here again you can repeat his 'Sit and stay' so that you can wait to cross the road safely. Impress on him that crossing a road is a matter of urgency and that he must not linger on the way over. Take the whole process of acclimatisation gently and keep talking to him in an encouraging manner, no matter how dotty passers-by think you are.

(I am, of course, assuming that his course of inoculations is complete before you venture outside the garden gate with him.)

Hopefully you will be able to train your Afghan to come to you on command. This requires a lot of patience and, with an Afghan, there is not a 100 per cent success rate. I never feel I can tell anyone it is safe to take one on a walk without a lead on a busy street. I am aware that some say they can but they are very definitely in the minority, and even though their dog regularly comes at a call his independent spirit could well cause him one day to dash off.

To train him initially to come on command, stand him in front of you on a long lead and you may find that the word 'Come!' backed up by a succulent titbit may be sufficient to bring your puppy flying towards you. If it does not work, haul him in gently towards you, repeating the command and praising him volubly as the required result is reached. Once more, do not overdo this. A few repeats with copious words of praise and a big cuddle at the end so that he realises that you are pleased with his efforts, even if it has not worked out entirely right first time, should gradually have the desired effect.

As he progresses repeat the exercise without a lead, so that he learns to come without physical control, and also increase the distance by using a piece of rope to hold him at a greater distance. As his obedience and understanding increases, it will be possible to dispense with the rope and then call him normally with a fair proportion of co-operation depending on how independent and intelligent he is. With luck you may find that in a playing field or park he may be fairly obedient but I advocate safety first: make sure that he is only allowed to run free in a well fenced enclosed space. Some Afghans never reach such a level of control, however hard you try. If they decide to abscond, you can chase and search for hours and the more you run after them the faster they gallop away. When this happens, the only thing to do is to sit down and find something around you highly interesting, and hope that his curiosity will get the better of him so that you can grasp his collar. Do not be embarrassed to sit on the path if necessary. Cunning and unconvention must be met with the same weapons.

Remember that whenever he is out of the garden your Afghan should wear a collar with his name attached. Contrary to general belief, it does not harm the coat. Many of us prefer the broad greyhound collar, built for a similar style of long, well muscled neck. This will sit firmly and not rub or tangle hair like a round collar or chain. A choke chain is useful for training, since you can so easily give a meaningful, restraining tug, and if you take your dog to training classes the instructor will possibly insist on the use of one of these collars while he is a member of the class. A long leather lead is more easily held, particularly with both hands simultaneously, which gives extra leverage and safety, than a very short strap or chain. Chains tend to be rather noisy and to my mind ruin the quiet, effortless grace and dignity so characteristic of the breed.

There are excellent training classes run by people devoted to canine affairs in most areas. Most dogs enjoy going to school and learn rapidly. The instructors will be glad to help you with a variety of problems and add polish to your initial training, such as by teaching you to bring your dog round you to heel from any position – a simple matter of placing your right foot behind you and rocking back on your heel while bringing your dog round behind you from the right side to the usual position on the left. Your dog is also taught to mingle with other dogs at very close quarters without interferring with them and in fact ignoring them. He will be taught to sit, lie and stand for minutes at a time and to behave when you are out of sight. You will also meet other dog owners and the evenings at classes pass quickly and pleasantly for you and the dog. In the process any anti-social tendencies in public will be neatly ironed out. However, once the retrieve and further training is reached it really no longer concerns you. He is a sight hound and was never meant to fetch and carry – in fact he finds no pleasure in doing so.

Since an Afghan puppy grows large quite rapidly you will find that a great many training classes that normally start dogs off at six months will accept Afghans. By their standards he is immature but the folk in charge do not always realise this. Your dog will not mind but may I suggest that at first you do not push his performance too hard. He is still, though needing training, very much a baby.

Since it is not always convenient to take your Afghan with you on some excursions – such as to the shops and the dentist – he must learn to behave sensibly when alone in the house. I do not advise leaving him to wander freely while still a puppy for all growing youngsters have a need to play and chew, and there are myriad temptations in any house. Anyway he is still too young to be a deterrent to any determined burglar. Put him in the kitchen where you keep his bed or in a light outhouse with his bed, toys, a bone and a drink and the always useful alarm clock. Even a transistor radio well out of his reach might be a comfort.

When you return, ignore the inevitable puddle but make it quite clear that you are as overjoyed to see him as he is to see you. Once he realises that there is always a loving reunion he will accept your absences with the fatalism that I always associate with these hairy animals. Try not to leave him so long that he starts to cry however, since the noise can become intolerable to even the most accommodating neighbours. In actual fact, if you are very sensible and accustom him to periods of being alone right from the start, he will learn to accept it just as he will accept being left alone at night.

Cars play an important part in the life of any Afghan who is to be a real companion to his owner. Take him for regular short journeys from the earliest days. At first he can cuddle up on someone's lap till he has accepted the motion and the unusual noise around him, then place him on the back seat or in the back of an estate car. His own blanket in the appropriate place will be useful since it represents security and normality. Encourage him to sleep while the car is in motion because on no account can he be allowed to leap about and distract the driver. A dog guard is most useful in an estate car.

On the whole it is inadvisable to feed him for several hours before a journey because sickness may result and if this happens on one of the first journeys it can easily become a bad habit. He must also be given a chance to relieve himself before the journey so that no guilt or worry can prey on his mind and ruin what should be a pleasant experience.

If your dog does turn out to be a definite dribbler and the first few journeys turn out to be a misery for both of you, obtain a very mild tranquilliser from the vet. After a few journeys with no ill-effects the dog will come to realise that there is no need for worry and begin to take travelling in his stride. I have also known of dogs not fond of cars being allowed to sit in a stationary one on the premises for a while before being given their favourite food while still sitting in it. Nevertheless for some dogs travel will always be an anathema and it should be realised that compared to our sheepdogs and terriers the Afghan veneer of 'civilisation' is still very thin and mentally they are still in the world of travel by horseback.

Try also to take him with you on a bus or train. There may be many an occasion when you find yourself unable to use your car when it is necessary that you and your dog travel together. Never shall I forget the terrible occasion when, travelling in a car of foreign make, it came to a grinding halt with no hope of spares and

TRAINING

I was left to travel from Birmingham to near the south coast of Kent with four large Afghans who had never seen a train in their lives. They worried, tugged, fretted and fumed and we all had a most miserable journey.

It must always be borne in mind that your dog is not naturally a blindly obedient dog as in the case of a retriever or spaniel, and any who fondly hope that they will 'master' their Afghan are not only due for bitter disappointment but are wickedly at fault in their attitude. His spirit must never be crushed to an obedient docility but he must be encouraged to co-operate. Each owner should learn to come to terms with their pet's own personality, and be prepared to outwit his basic cunning.

You may realise that all this attention to making your dog a civilised hound is going to take far more time than you can adequately spare. In that case it is far better not to have him in the first place. Untrained he will be a most frustrating dog, not even at peace with himself, and most certainly not a social companion. Trained he will be a humourous, affectionate, loyal and delightful friend.

The result is in *your* hands.

3
Care and Management

Although a grown Afghan – or indeed any Afghan from a few months old – is quite a tough fellow, he does nevertheless need quite a lot of day-to-day care. He must be groomed, regularly fed and thoroughly exercised: a flabby, out-of-condition Afghan is a sad sight, and a bored Afghan is a mischievous creature who must somehow divest himself of excess energy. This usually takes the form of chewing either furniture, carpets, doors and window frames, or, most upsetting of all, his own beautiful coat. I intend therefore to set out the daily needs of the average dog of this breed as simply as possible, as well as simple information on the things which can occur to the most beautifully maintained dog.

Feeding

As probably the subject most dear to the Afghan heart, and his source of life and health, we will consider this first. Once out of puppyhood your dog will probably become a one-meal-a-day dog with a drink of milk to which is added an egg. Provided that he has his vitamin capsule daily – or whatever other means you take of giving him his dietary supplement – he will do very well indeed on a simple diet. He does not need rich meat, and too many sweet titbits will cause him to be overweight and damage his teeth. Meat that can be chewed to exercise the jaws, a good grade of hound meal or large crunchy wholemeal biscuit that will supply roughage and a general conditioner such as Canovel, Vetzyme or Linetone, and little else is needed.

An elderly and possibly old-fashioned vet with a great deal of practical knowledge of rearing and feeding many breeds of dogs, suggested stewing up my dogs' meat with vegetables and garlic and making a good rich gravy at the same time. This stew, with the meat chopped up to bite-sized pieces, was then mixed with a similar quantity of meal consisting of 50 per cent biscuit meal, 25 per cent flaked maize and 25 per cent rolled oats. The whole amount was mixed together with the gravy to the consistency of a crumbly cake. My dogs used to wolf this down and any cod-liver oil, wheat-germ oil or bone flour was very easily mixed in and assimilated.

This same vet also introduced me to nettles when I complained about a bitch's nose going pinkish in colour during a very long cold winter. They are a prolific source of copper and, when tender young nettles are boiled, they turn out very similar to spinach.

They can be collected in spring and early summer and the liquor obtained after boiling stored in glass containers. Dosage with the nettle tea — 1 dessertspoonful daily — assured me of excellent pigmentation throughout the kennel and added an excellent tonic.

Garlic is reputed to be of inestimable value in the general conditioning of your Afghan and can be administered either in tablet form from such firms as Denes Veterinary Products or the National Rearing Products or by the simple expedient of adding a crushed clove of garlic when cooking the food. This flavour really does appeal to the Afghan. Conditions helped by the administration of garlic are worms, diarrhoea and coughs, but basically, like onions, it is an excellent internal cleanser. Seaweed powder added to the feed also helps to condition a poor coat. Some schools of thought even recommend a complete turnover to herbal feeding and state that only raw meat should be fed — a reproduction of the dog's diet in the wild.

Unfortunately many people find it easier to just slip the Afghan a few proprietary conditioning tablets, but the use of some natural products has excellent results as I have personally found.

The most ardent exponent of natural rearing is Juliette de Baraclai Levy, now residing in Palestine, who will be remembered through her Turkuman kennel name. She has reared litters using herbs and raw meat and has stated what wonderfully strong dogs she has produced.

It is often just as difficult to fatten up a thin dog as it is to slim an obese one. In fact it is often even more difficult, since it is largely a matter of a dog's basic metabolism and some burn up their food at a colossal rate. Every kennel has its own pet remedies which vary from giving a tablespoon of lard or dripping to mixing fish oil or linseed oil in its meal. I always add potatoes and give several meals a week which include that rather fatty meat, breast of lamb. If it does not add any appreciable flesh to the bones, I usually find they have a good general condition with a rich glossy coat and muzzle. Also extra drinks of milk never come amiss and these skinny ones should definitely be kept on breakfast as well as fed twice a day, instead of once only. It is also necessary to increase their intake of vitamins D, B and K as well as calcium.

Slimming is, of course, slightly harrowing since dogs take such pleasure in their food, but the major part of the fat dog's meal should take the form of red meat with no fat, water to drink and a lot of cuddles to make up for the comfort of the food he is missing. Add a general conditioner and hopefully he will become a normal size of hound. This is far better for his general health and condition, particularly since an Afghan is built for running over difficult terrain and his heart and lungs were never meant to carry an excess of fat.

Obesity can also be caused by a malfunctioning thyroid gland; sometimes this is also accompanied by a slightly bulging eyeball and occasionally a cataract.

Give your dog some variety in his food, if only as a matter of expediency. You do not want him to refuse liver because he is used to beef steak and you don't happen to have any in the house on a Bank Holiday weekend. Variety also keeps him interested and on his toes at feeding time. Beef, not necessarily the expensive cuts, but shin of beef or brisket, is an excellent food as the dog grows, so are ox cheek and lips. Breast of lamb, particularly if rubbed over with garlic or garlic salt and then grilled, is an absolute delight and dogs will crunch through chunks of it (soft bones also) with an expression of utter ecstasy. This particular meat is very good for the thin dog but is rather rich and should not be fed continuously. Liver should be given only once a week as it tends to make them rather loose but is therefore a useful cleanser for the stomach. Melt has an even more obvious effect and, although cheap, we always try to avoid it.

Lamb has a flavour that really appeals to the Afghan (shades of Kipling's 'Cinnamon stew of the fat-tailed sheep') but all the bones should be removed after stewing. The paunches of pigs, sheep and liver are other valuable feeds if obtainable. Straight from the slaughter house they are a revolting sight and the smell defies description. However, they are an animal's natural food and the part always eaten first after a dog has hunted and killed. They contain many natural minerals and it is unfortunate that few of us nowadays are able to obtain this wonderful source of food. It is possible to feed them cooked or raw but if cooked the gravy should not be used for its richness could make a dog exceedingly loose in its motions. If fed raw the dog should be checked and, if necessary, dosed for tapeworm regularly, say every six months. Chicken is a great favourite and is wonderful for dogs that need a fat-free diet, or for invalids. Under no circumstances, however, should they be allowed to crunch up the brittle bones, since these can penetrate the stomach lining — and so also can rabbit bones.

Fish is excellent for invalids or for Afghans who are temporarily off their food. We get a wonderful rich fish locally called huss. It is a long fish with a central bone similar to an eel. Avoid very bony fish however as there can be the odd accident with fish bones in the throat.

In all feeding, however, there is a basic requirement. The Afghan must be able to chew and to exercise his powerful jaw. Soft proprietary foods are useless for keeping those strong white teeth in good condition and in the wild he would have torn his prey to pieces, fur, bones and all. One must never lose sight of an Afghan hound's origin, since it is all related to his care and maintenance.

Milk is good for all dogs, young or old unless their diet is specifically fat free and is, of course, a prime source of calcium.

Drinking

Always make sure that your Afghan has a clean bowl of fresh water whenever he wishes and, as many Afghans have a strange habit of actually bathing and paddling in their water trough, you may find it necessary to wash and refill it several times a day. I own a most elegant black dog who spends the greater part of any hot day curled up in the full water trough in the run and actually goes to sleep there with his head supported on the side to the great frustration of his fellows, who find it impossible to drink without getting their noses tangled in black fur.

Exercise

This is the other great interest in an Afghan's life. If it is impossible to allow him to stretch his legs during the day in some way then please don't have him at all. A slack-muscled Afghan is a most dejected creature and he does not move nicely, becomes overweight and lethargic, and is never in the peak of condition, besides being plain bored.

Wherever possible give him ample running space, fenced off so that he can tear around to his heart's content without spoiling your lawns and flower beds and where, if the fit so takes him, he can dig out all those strange earthworks of such enormous appeal to his devious mind and which actually go round corners so that he can lurk completely out of sight.

Not only should the dog run free but he should be walked daily to accustom him to roads, traffic and people. The length of these walks depends upon the amount of free exercise he has each day but he does need at least a mile a day of steady walking. This exercise at a steady pace is unsurpassed for keeping a dog at the peak of muscular condition. If you really cannot find a place suitable to let your dog off the lead, without his being able to get onto a road or into the fields with sheep, I suggest that you let him gallop away from you on a long length of nylon line attached to his collar. This allows him quite a lot of freedom to gambol and he will soon learn to play and run within its limits without coming to a sudden jerk at the end of his line. I do not advocate just tying him to a long length of rope in the garden under any circumstances – that is asking for trouble. He can become hopelessly entangled or end up pathetically pulling at his line because it does not solve his need for combined exercise, fun and companionship.

Some Afghans seem to have a built-in laziness factor nevertheless and however frequently you put them out to play they can be found quietly snoozing beneath their favourite bush. With these it is just sheer hard labour on their owner's part that keeps them mobile. The purchase of a companion may inspire them to take more exercise.

America has produced several patent dog exercisers to which the dog is fastened and taken round in a wide circle at a steady pace, on a mechanised lead and there is also quite a lot of exercising done by taking a dog behind a bike on quiet roads – quite a sensible method of keeping him fit while still retaining the human element.

CARE AND MANAGEMENT

Grooming

This is a serious and necessary part of your pet's maintenance and is a definite chore that cannot be neglected if you value his coat and welfare.

Always, when your Afghan comes home after his daily jaunt, it will be necessary to carry out a detailed search into his coat to remove any leaves, twigs or seeds that have become entangled, as well as cleaning up his paws which will be either tangled, dusty, muddy or just plain soaking wet. Mud and sticky dirt will entail standing each paw in turn in a bowl of water and washing. Plain dust and dry dirt can be brushed out of the whole coat when it has been well and truly cleaned with talcum powder. This makes a cheap dry shampoo and coat sweetener when rubbed in well, after which the dog is stood over a piece of newspaper and then brushed out. You will be surprised at the colour of the talcum powder

A standing dog being groomed layer by layer. In this case the back leg has been groomed starting at the bottom until only the top layer remains (*Kent Studios*)

when it comes out while the coat will be left soft and silky.

Twigs, particularly thorny ones, can very easily get caught up in the long coat and must be carefully disentangled. Most of them tend to roll themselves up with the coat acting like a bandage. The technique therefore is to unroll them carefully and avoid any tearing.

Seeds can be caught up equally quickly, particularly in the groin and the armpit. It is therefore always necessary to run your hand underneath the dog and into all his nooks and crannies, or else to train him to be groomed lying on his side so that it is possible to lift his legs and see what is nestling underneath.

There are two schools of thought about grooming. Some people like to train their dog to stand still on a bench while the hair is lifted upward. They then groom by taking the bottom layer around the feet first, giving it a thorough groom, and then work their way upward and all over the dog, layer by layer (see illustration). This is particularly effective at shows, where a dog is expected to step straight from his grooming table and (hopefully) into the ring with an immaculate coat. It is essential that the section between the hind legs is not missed out, but with a well trained dog this is quite feasible. It is also necessary to make sure that you have a regular grooming pattern. I always start at the hindlegs with a standing dog, work along the flank and back and then do the neck and head, ears and then the foreleg and front. Other people start at the head.

The other method of grooming and in my opinion the most successful ever, if you have a large enough space, is to lay your dog on his side with his back towards you and to start grooming by layering his hair towards you from the backbone, brushing it backwards about an inch at a time (see illustration). This enables you to see anything caught up in the coat and any incipient mats, very easily.

After the whole body has been dealt with in this way the coat is then brushed downwards back into position, and your dog is ready for any conditioner or spray that you wish to use. As you progress to the legs they can be dealt with in the same way, so that the inner leg is exposed for grooming and the area inside the groin can be in-

The inside of the hind leg is being groomed. It is easy to remove knots etc from the groin in this position (*Kent Studios*)

With the dog lying down facing away from the handler, the coat is brushed back in approximately one-inch layers exposing all knots and foreign bodies (*Kent Studios*)

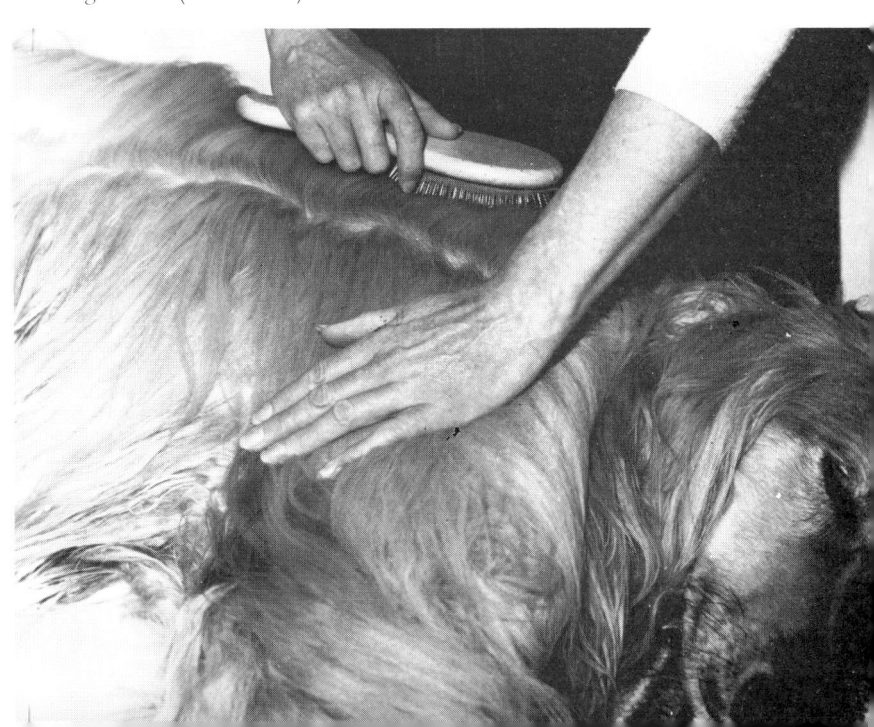

spected for foreign bodies (see illustration). Any sticky knots around the penis and testicles can be trimmed away since a dog is prone to lick and nibble in this area. In the event that you have a mat or even a mere suggestion of one, work it apart with your fingers little by little, doing your best to avoid pulling out any coat, and then brush through with a wire brush. Hair that comes out will probably only be dead hair that caused matting in the first place and would come out with grooming anyway.

There are various proprietary sprays for use on a groomed coat to give gloss, substance and, supposedly, to deter knots. A slightly oily one does help to reduce the flyaway tendency of so many coats, but nothing will compare with the texture and shine of really good health and regular brushing.

During your daily grooming session, which need not be at all a lengthy business if your dog is brushed regularly and kept in sparkling condition, you should examine his paws for foreign bodies and knots between the toes, see that his claws are not overlong and look inside his ears to see that there is no wax or any sign of a seed tucked inside the ear-flap. Quite obviously it will be very noticeable if he has a sticky or runny eye or runny nose. In the case of a bitch there should also be a regular quick check to see that there is no unexpected vaginal discharge or, when a season is approaching, to see whether there are any signs of its imminence.

Bathing is necessary (apart from being the inevitable preliminary to a show) only when the dog is dirty or smelly, for it tends to remove the natural oils from a coat and these will then need replacing. Before the bath groom the coat out well, making sure that every knot is gone so that they are not washed and tangled in more deeply. Use a good brand of dog shampoo (nowadays excellent ones are made for the soft Afghan coat) and mix according to instructions. Stand the dog in the bath, having already started your spray running with the water mixed to a gentle warmth, not too cold, but not hot enough to scald a skin which, unlike ours, is not used to regular immersion in hot water. Spray the side nearest to you until it is really wet (I should wet one side only first and avoid the dog having to stand around all cold and clammy as far as possible). Rub in the shampoo gently but thoroughly, trying to tangle the hair as little as possible. Then rinse out and apply a second coat, rubbing it in as before. Do avoid getting any water or shampoo in the eyes and be careful with the spray around his topknot so that you do not upset him unduly. They are very sensitive about having water around their hair and faces.

Rinse out the shampoo really well, pushing your hand downwards with the water and so smoothing out any lather that may be lingering. Then complete the second side and make very sure that you washed his 'shirt front' and the portion under the tail which may have become soiled. After this use a coat conditioner, which, when well rubbed in, must be left for several minutes before being rinsed out thoroughly. Do take pains over your rinsing or you will be left with some sticky patches. Then wring out your dog's coat in sections, gently; under no circumstances must you pull the hair and hurt him since a bath should as far as possible be a pleasure in which a dog can enjoy being fussed over by his owner; it must not turn into a punishment.

The dog will undoubtedly help to rid its coat of surplus water by shaking all over, ending with that endearing Afghan quirk, a subtle shake of its tail. Mop up as much excess water as possible with a towel then brush your Afghan through to make sure that no knots have formed during the inevitable handling of the coat. After that, brush the hair in several directions downwards and sideways under a warm blast from a hair-dryer. This virtually gives a blow dry and leaves the coat soft, silky, straight and manageable.

If you do not have a hair-dryer, give as much gentle drying as possible with the towel, groom him out thoroughly and then put him in a warm room near a radiator. Brush his coat through gently every half hour or so, at the same time doing any further work necessary with a towel, and he will take from two to three hours to dry thoroughly. Then give a final groom over and a coat spray. At all costs avoid getting a wet Afghan into a cold draught.

Remember too that it always pays to put a snood over your Afghan's head while it is eating so that there are no tasty little snacks of meat or gravy tucked away on the ear fringes for a midnight feast (see illustration). So many long ear fringes have been

A snood provides excellent protection for ear fringes during feeding (*Kent Studios*)

chewed off in that way. The snood takes the form of a tube about 15in long, either elasticated or of a stretch fabric, or even just a length cut from an old nylon stocking.

Bugs

However carefully your pet is looked after, Afghan coats are a boon to the marauding flea or louse, lurking in wait on a fence-post, tree or in the grass to find just such an accommodating, fluffy host. A flea in an Afghan's coat is certainly not a major disgrace but everyone should take precautions to ensure that the occasion cannot arise since fleas and lice carry germs and can be responsible for tapeworm infestation. Powder your dog regularly, therefore, with a strong louse powder, preferably one made for farm animals, not pet pussies. These preparations, which can be bought from any farm and garden suppliers, smell like river sludge, but they are exceedingly effective. Rub the powder firmly into the coat, right down to the skin and particularly behind the ears and the elbows where there are cosy corners for these wretched creatures to breed and attach their eggs safely in hard cemented clusters. Repeat this process every two weeks and you will kill off both the living parasites and the hatching eggs. This is a precaution which will be necessary throughout a warm season and, incidentally, all the year round if you live in the country where hedgehogs and foxes abound. In the event of a bad infestation there are also various shampoos, some obtainable from your vet, which give very good results, although the coat looks drab, slightly sticky and unkempt during the interval between the shampoos.

Sleeping accommodation

Having fed, exercised and groomed your dog, you must finally see that his night's rest is sound and undisturbed. His sleeping quarters should always be in a draught-free cosy spot. The bed should be raised several inches from the ground with a back and side pieces to keep any little breezes from him and he will need a mattress or blanket. A young Afghan does not need an expensive basket or bed to start with as he will in all probability chew it up. A strong wooden or cardboard box will suffice at first, as long as it keeps him in a warm position. It is also a place where he can retire for a peaceful rest away from the family with his own toys and blanket and should be respected as such.

He will happily sleep in a kitchen with a boiler, or in a room left at a temperature of around 60° but if he is to obtain the maximum benefit from his food and sleep, particularly when he is a growing puppy he should not have to waste all his energy engendering warmth and fighting off the cold. Also, bearing in mind that he is one of the family, he must not be tucked away in an outhouse at the bottom of the garden. This will lead to distress and insecurity and also a tendency to howl and bark during the night at any marauding mouse that passes.

As he grows he can graduate to a comfortable sound bed or one of those elegant folding 'settees' which is a really accommodating piece of furniture and which does seem to appeal to the Afghan taste.

4
Sickness and Old Age

Sickness

If you are lucky, your dog will sail through life with nothing worse than puppy teething troubles and the odd cut paw and sprain, but always remember that, if anything about his health puzzles you, your vet is undoubtedly your best friend with a reliable Afghan breeder a close second.

Worming
Worming is necessary for a young puppy, first at the age of three weeks and then every two weeks until the infestation is cleared. After that he can usefully be wormed every six months for the remainder of his life.

A common symptom of worm infestation is diarrhoea and a patchy-looking coat (the latter being particularly noticeable in a puppy). There may be a cough and in extreme youth a distension of the stomach. A badly infested dog will squat on the ground and drag his bottom along to relieve the irritation. The usual ones found in the Afghan puppy are roundworms and, sometimes, hookworms. They are small thread-like creatures, which at times appear in the faeces in horrible pale clusters. Less common is the tapeworm, which requires special dosage and appears as flat white segments adhering to the coat. Both worms, but in particular the tapeworm, can cause severe debility and in the case of the young puppy even death.

Inoculation
Inoculation (with a killed vaccine) is one of the essentials in a dog's

life. This will protect him from hard pad, distemper, hepatitis and leptospirosis, all singularly nasty killers in their own way. Each year he needs a booster injection. You will find that if you wish to board your dog all reputable kennels insist on seeing the certificate and will refuse to take him without it. This attitude protects both your dog and the other boarders.

Always insist that the viral hepatitis vaccine is a dead one since live vaccines have been known to cause a condition known as blue eye in the Afghan and some other breeds. This causes blindness and disfigurement. Apart from these arguments it is vitally necessary for his own sake that he is protected from these avoidable but lethal diseases.

In the States there is yet another hazard, heartworm, which is also rife in Australia. Once more inoculation is the only safe way to avoid unnecessary death.

SICKNESS AND OLD AGE

Ear conditions
Afghans are distinctly prone to excessively waxy ears which, unless promptly dealt with and regularly treated, can become seriously inflamed and blocked, ulcerated, smelly and sometimes bad enough to warrant a resection. One contributory factor is the heavy hairy flap that hangs down over the actual orifice and keeps cool fresh air out and heat, dirt and germs enclosed. At least a weekly clean out is necessary, with damp cotton wool wound over the end of a pair of tweezers, to combat any tendency to these troubles. Care must be taken that no sharp points can penetrate the tender lining of the ear and cleaning must be a very gentle undertaking. Soothing drops to soften hard wax and cure inflammation are available from your vet, whose advice should always be sought in difficult or worrying cases. The older dog may have more problems still with his ears as a result of polyps, which can cause bleeding as well as excess wax.

Parasites also can creep into the ears; little mites can cause a huge amount of trouble and again can demand the services of your vet.

If, however, your dog seems to have only a little rather hard wax in his ears causing irritation, warm olive oil dropped in with a dropper and left there for an hour or two will soften it before cleaning with cotton wool.

Eyes
On the whole Afghans suffer from nothing more than an occasional cold in the eyes or slight infections which can be cleaned up with the appropriate ointment. It is always a good thing to keep a dosage for simple ailments like this in your medicine chest. We always keep neomycin ointment from the vet in the medicine chest. A tube should not be kept for more than a month, once opened.

There are, however, one or two unpleasant conditions which your dog could acquire or inherit. The most common is the pink haw, an enlargement of the third eyelid, a gland at the inner corner of the eye. This commonly spreads over the eye in sleep and then retracts again but can be larger than usual in one or both eyes giving a most unAfghan-like expression. Your vet will advise on treatment of this condition but it must be remembered that, if he advises a cosmetic operation, Kennel Club rules frown very heavily on any form of faking.

A condition, entropion, can arise from hereditary causes, accident or even a foreign body embedded under the eyelid. This is commonly known as ingrowing eyelids and is a most painful condition that will close a dog's eye, cause ulceration to the eyeball and is curable only by a surgical operation.

If your dog is unfortunate enough to need treatment involving an irritable condition or stitching to the face or ears, a plastic bucket with the bottom removed and holes pierced around the base so that it may be attached to the collar will enable him to heal without his being able to worry at it with his paws.

Blocked anal glands
If your pet shows signs of discomfort and nibbles himself raw under his tail, consult your vet without delay. It is probable that his anal glands have become blocked and a simple matter for your vet to clear them in minutes. Do not attempt to squeeze them out yourself unless you have been thoroughly instructed in the correct method by the vet. This is a condition more commonly found in the young dog, who usually grows out of it.

Diarrhoea
This can have various causes. A dog undergoing a change of surroundings, air, diet and water can become very loose but if there is no other cause present, apart from excitement, a very simple remedy is to add a dessertspoonful of cornflour to his food. An upset tummy caused by a mild germ will need dosing with kaolin and antibiotics. Remember also that a dog can get a chill through being allowed in a draught with a wet coat.

If, during an attack of diarrhoea, your dog passes blood in any form whatever consult your vet immediately, since it could be the symptom of one of the particularly virulent types of enteritis which can cause havoc in the canine world. This happens particularly in the middle of a bad winter, also during hot weather when flies abound and settle in the dog runs. It can also be symptomatic of distemper-based germs.

Dick and Marcia Stoll of the Dicmar kennel, California. Dick handles the superb smoky blue Ch Tajmirs Gunsmoke of Mecca while Marcia handles Gunsmoke's daughter Ch Dicmar's Blue Dhimond. The author was privileged to judge Gunsmoke in America and found him, even at the age of eleven, in excellent hard condition showing like a much younger dog (*Twomey*)

Teeth

When your puppy is born he is toothless and then develops small, singularly sharp, needle-like baby teeth. From around the age of ten weeks he starts to shed these and an adult set of forty-two teeth gradually emerges. There is of course always a chance that your Afghan may be one in which a premolar is missing but if his breeding has been carefully thought out and his rearing has been scrupulous he should be perfect in his dentition. To keep these teeth in excellent condition it is essential that he has a hard bone to gnaw regularly and at least one partially crispy meal daily in order to keep his gums hard and his teeth free from tartar. If tartar does form then a special instrument for carefully scraping it from the surface of the tooth may be purchased from most dog suppliers.

In appearance it is like a small curved chisel but great care must be taken that in levering off lumps of tartar the enamel is not damaged. Since it is a very awkward operation you should if at all doubtful consult your vet, particularly if you feel that there may be decay present as well. In the case of a very stubborn dog, that hates having any attention to its mouth or who has developed a really painful condition due to a build-up of tartar, an anaesthetic may be necessary.

If a tooth becomes hopelessly decayed and painful, particularly in the older dog, the vet can extract it under a general anaesthetic. Roots can be large and deepset with a correspondingly large hole remaining but the operation is straightforward and sensible soft meals and cossetting will speed recovery. On no account must he suffer agonising toothache.

Foot care
Toe nails can sometimes be a nuisance if your dog spends most of his time playing on grass rather than walking on hard pavement. His nails can be cut, but only with a proper pair of clippers. Care must be taken not to cut the nail too short and so damage the quick, and the paw must be held very firmly, otherwise a mistake can be made when a worried dog pulls his paw away or leaps about. If you find this is too difficult for you, a breeder, dog beautician or vet will help.

The dew claws a little further up the front leg will most probably have been removed when your Afghan was only about three or four days old, in which case there will be only a residual pad on the foreleg, but if not, do make sure that the nail is not growing too long, since without attention they sometimes tend to curl back towards the flesh. If they are ever badly caught during more active moments then they can be quite nastily torn and painful, but by this time it will need an operation under anaesthetic to remove them. The dew claws are the fifth digit (or thumb) when the puppies are born and only have soft, flat, unformed little paws. As the foot grows, so they acquire their position further up the leg. They should be removed by clipping off the whole of the digit at the top join three days after birth by the vet – not yourself. He just gives a sharp snip and the offending claw is gone. The small raw patch is then dabbed with a potassium permanganate solution, if bleeding occurs, and all is over.

Paws are very prone to injury since, despite the protection of their very tough, slightly rough pads, the Afghan does a great deal of digging, running, jumping and even climbing. (I have two who regularly climb a beech tree to find a different run or even to just come visiting to the house.) The first sign of a cut pad is usually a bloody paw mark and possibly a limp. Immediately wash the paw in a gentle disinfectant solution and, once clean, examine it carefully to find and remove foreign bodies. If necessary, clip away any hair that can get into the wound. Pad the cut firmly with a piece of lint treated with antiseptic ointment and make sure that it is thick and tight enough to staunch the bleeding. Cover the pad with a wad of cotton wool and bandage firmly well up the leg. I always keep a supply of old socks which can be fitted over the paw like a bag and then taped firmly around wrist or ankle. A polythene bag may be placed over the dressing before a dog is taken out into the rain but this must not be kept on indefinitely because it retains heat and moisture.

If the wound is very deep and wide you must go to your vet as in all probability stitching will be needed. To stop bleeding it may be necessary to use a tourniquet over the vein or artery. Remember to apply the tourniquet between the wound and the heart side if an artery is cut but on the side farthest from the heart if it is a vein.

False pregnancies
Bitches are somewhat prone to this condition and can make themselves positively ill about nine weeks after the time they would have been mated. They may produce a considerable quantity of milk and are able to feed puppies that need fostering should they be so inclined. This milk must be dispersed with prescribed tablets and also make sure that the bitch does not drink too much milk. Although the dosing with Epsom salts has been recommended as a cure for this condition for many years by breeders, it is not good

for the bitch as it causes diarrhoea and a definite tendency toward dehydration.

One of the symptoms of a false pregnancy is the incredible amount of digging in the carpet when everyone else is preparing to go to bed, a making of beds behind chairs and a continual fretting and mournful howling. They will actually go through all the motions of having puppies, puffing, panting, licking themselves, crooning to their imaginary babes and refusing to get up to leave their make-believe litters. When they do leave them there is a frantic search on their return because they are sure that they really exist but that they have somehow carelessly mislaid them. One of my bitches prone to this condition regularly 'produces' at least nine puppies for several nights after every season and causes me some very disturbed nights. She is slightly comforted when I give her a woolly to cuddle.

If you are not interested in showing, most vets will advise that a bitch of this type is spayed. This usually clears up the trouble and helps some of the worst cases who become terribly upset internally. In the case of a show bitch, however, this is not permissible — if you wish to continue showing her — unless she has already gained her title, has won her way into the stud book or has produced progeny themselves entered in the stud book.

There are snags to spaying, since some bitches tend to put on extra weight, and there is also a strong tendency to grow the facial 'puppy whiskers' once more.

Mammary tumours
These form in the teats, sometimes in the form of hard, granulated lumps (often the result of undissolved milk secretions during a false pregnancy) or as a complete enlargement of the whole gland as in pregnancy. It frequently occurs in older bitches and vets often recommend spaying as well as the removal of the tumour.

Do not neglect to obtain treatment for this conditon under the mistaken idea that it is an immediate death sentence; tumours are frequently benign and such operations can be carried out to an advanced age.

Hernias
Umbilical hernias look like a soft bubble on the abdomen of the puppy. They can be caused through a hard pull on the cord during whelping but there can also be hereditary factors involved. Small ones are not dangerous and can safely be ignored but if they are larger than ½in your puppy should have a minor operation.

Skin troubles
An Afghan usually has a healthy, if occasionally dry skin. He can nevertheless develop a very nasty rash under his tummy if he is allowed to get too wet and muddy and is then not adequately cleaned and dried, so that his coat, rubbing against the skin, almost flays it, causing dreadful pain. In these cases the skin becomes inflamed and stiff and he must be anointed gently with a cooling antiseptic ointment and may even need sedating for you to be able to treat it at all.

Eczema
This is a term widely used to cover various forms of inflammation and must be treated by a vet, who will make the initial diagnosis.

Mange
This is contagious and on no account should a dog with this condition be allowed to mix with others. It is usually characterised by severe irritation on the face, limbs and brisket. Once more, it must be treated professionally.

Sprains
These are not unusual in an active youngster but somewhat less common in an adult whose limbs are under superb control. The symptoms are usually a loud and prolonged screaming, a limping dog holding the offending limb up, and a rather hot joint. If you are quite certain that nothing is broken, the best remedy is lots of rest and regular administration of hot and cold compresses.

Broken limbs
Will undoubtedly cause a great deal of pain, probably a limpness

of the affected limb with complete loss of use, and in many cases the structure of the break is obvious. You cannot possibly deal with this yourself but try to keep the dog as immobile as possible.

Rickets
If your puppy is well reared from the start, there should be no occurrence of this devastating, painful condition, but in the event of a calcium deficiency it becomes very obvious that one or more joints are affected, since they become swollen and painful. In extreme cases whole bone shafts – for example the forelegs – can become bent and ribs will become knobbly. An immediate steady administration of calcium in the form of bone flour or calcium phosphate must commence, and a consultation with the vet will doubtless include booster vitamin D injections. The puppy must be rested and in severe cases his joints may have to be strapped to prevent further damage. There is sometimes an occurrence of the condition in a young dog after injury and always, if a bone is badly bruised or a leg severely damaged, step up the calcium for a few days.

Pancreatic trouble
This is a condition rapidly becoming more identified in our breed. It may be that we have unknowingly suffered from it for many years without realising what it was, only realising that a dog was a 'poor doer'. It is actually caused by a deficiency of pancreatic enzymes causing incomplete digestion of food so that the dog receives very little nutriment as a result. He will become morbidly thin with a poor coat and will suffer from an offensive, discoloured diarrhoea. He will also become an easy prey for worms. Upon positive diagnosis he will immediately be put upon a fat-free diet and dosed with pancreatic enzymes. Simple nourishing fat-free feeding can be achieved by giving boiled chicken or fish, instead of a stronger meat, and rice instead of biscuit. If the rice seems rather dreary for the dog it can be cooked with seasoned chicken broth from which the fat has been strained, or with a gravy powder with garlic added.

Periods of such feeding, and quantities, vary with the dog. Some need it all their lives; others for limited periods occasionally. However, no longer need one despair over a dog that seems to be fading away for no apparent reason.

Temperatures
A vital thing to know about the general maintenance of your dog is how to take its temperature, for this can be of prime importance in so many conditions.

It is quite possible that you may need a helper to hold the dog, since it tends to consider, quite rightly, that the whole process is a violation of its privacy. Shake the thermometer to bring it down to 95 ° F, dip the end in petroleum jelly, then gently slide the thermometer into the rectum for about 1in, allowing it to find its own angle. Hold it there for 1 to 2min. The normal temperature is 101.3°F; over 102.5° is regarded as a high temperature worth veterinary attention, but remember an excited dog may have a slightly higher temperature than normal.

Hereditary conditions
These are fortunately comparatively few in the Afghan and are also, unfortunately, rather hidden under the carpet in many quarters where stud interests are high and puppy sales at a premium.

Hip dysplasia
Was at one time the bugbear of the Afghan population when suddenly discovered to be rife in English dogs and not, as smugly supposed, contained on the other side of the world. America recognised the problem many years ago and organised a great deal of research into the subject while reputable breeders checked their dogs with X-rays. When attending a canine symposium in California in 1967 my husband, mentioning that English dogs were clear of the affliction had a sharp retort from a well known breeder who said, 'What do you mean you don't have it. Don't have it or don't look?' Taken aback he had to admit that nobody looked and shortly afterwards Miss Kean and Miss McKenzie bravely informed the Afghan world that a well known imported dog which they owned was suffering from this condition and advised

that all his stock be checked. Sure enough, some had it and as a result a great many of us mended our ways, had our dogs X-rayed and some surprising results among superb movers were uncovered. This condition – which is a flattening or mis-shaping of the head of the femur and a flattening or shallowness of the socket in which it lies – is definitely something it is inadvisable to 'double up' when breeding, but as its clinical effects on the Afghan, because of its strong muscular loin and lack of excessive weight behind, are not as disastrous as in other breeds, it is no longer considered a reason for panic hysteria. Nevertheless, it can cause a painful arthritic condition in some older dogs. One of mine found to be badly affected on one side developed rheumatism at the age of eleven and a tendency to have a slightly unsound appearance in the affected leg. Symptoms of hip dysplasia can also be found after an accident where a young puppy has had to walk awkwardly on a joint when the bones were in a formative period. It cannot be adequately proven in a dog until he is a year old.

Juvenile cataract
This usually becomes obvious at the age of 12 to 18 months. It can cause blindness or can clear itself.

Progressive retinal atrophy
This can now be checked from the age of one year onwards and there is a British veterinary scheme under which dogs can be tested. It is hoped this will weed out affected stock. Fortunately the incidence in Afghans is low.

Old age and parting

Afghans remain remarkably youthful throughout their lives, and apart from greyness round the muzzle age little from 5 to 10. Readers may remember the spectacular entrance made by an eleven-year old in the Open Class at Crufts 1976, when Ch Ranjitsinhji of Jagai showed with the verve, condition and fullness of coat that made him winner of the Hound Group and third Best in Show at Crufts 1969.

Your dog needs regular exercise to keep his muscles trim, since

One of the author's hounds—a striking pure black, Ch Begum Kanda of Jagai, whose mother was imported from Holland (*Shadwell*)

fatness can lead to problems with heart and lungs, although as age increases length of walks decreases. Similarly diet should aim to avoid obesity; if necessary feed liberally with protein in the form of meat and vegetable and cut down on biscuit.

Even when his vigour diminishes and he is no longer an energetic hound but a dear cuddly creature pottering around his domain, I trust you will still value your Afghan's life as long as he is still happy, carefree and dignified. He will be perfectly content in his continued existence as long as he feels no pain or discomfort and is with his family.

No dog should be disposed of because of increasing age or expense; when you first took him into your family it should have been implicit that his privilege to live his life to a peaceful and fulfilled conclusion would be safeguarded. Nevertheless when, for one reason or another, his life has become a burden to him, or if he becomes unavoidably undignified or incontinent in his habits then grant him the privilege of death with dignity. Do not let him eke out a wretched existence with rapidly failing faculties because you cannot bear to part with him. This is not love, but selfishness. You are responsible for his well being which must come before your own feelings; if loneliness is feared there are always sad Afghans without homes on various club rescue schemes.

It is of necessity a sad occasion but do not transmit that feeling to your dog, who must not leave this life with any feeling of distress or worry. Nor should he have to make the journey to the surgery but meet his ending in his own home. Make him comfortable in his own bed, or put his blanket under him on his favourite patch of the settee. If he hates injections give a tablet sedative so that he can drowse off to sleep with you before the vet's arrival.

Giving him perpetual sleep is not a grim, unpleasant experience, merely putting a rather large injection directly into a vein and he will know nothing, only that you are there cuddling him. Talk to him for those few seconds and save your tears until he is gone; a small effort for one who has given you so much pleasure. If you cannot face it let one of his best friends be present who can, but, please, do not let him go in an unhappy atmosphere.

It is worth realising that dogs do not appear to approach their end with the foreboding common to most humans. I feel that their understanding of these matters is far greater than ours.

Death is not always a matter of great unhappiness either. Sometimes they slip quietly away in their sleep and some even leave in an atmosphere of enjoyment while living their life to the full. I think here of the end of one of the breed's great stud dogs, Champion Pasha of Carloway, who ended his days as a valued companion in our establishment. He was an absolute sweetheart, cuddly, gentle, a martinet with the bitches whom he used as cushions at night and who finally became a sweet-loving old gentleman with a very weak heart. To safeguard his health he was given his own private quarters and here, one tremendously hot summer's day, when the thirteen-year old Pasha was dozing in the shade, came his daughter who later became Champion Begum Kanda of Jagai. She was jet black with paws like a monkey and it was easy work for her to push the bolt on his door aside, entice the old stud dog out and insist that he mate her. My husband found them together and carried the exhausted Pasha to a shady tree where he lay recovering with a cool drink. Kanda was shut indoors in disgrace.

Kanda, being, I am convinced, a true specimen of a 'Hanuman dog', managed to open a door and make her way through the house to an open window. From there it was easy to find Pasha and appeal once more to his baser instincts. He was found with her — limp but obviously proud of his achievements so in character with the rest of his life. He was carried to his kennel and laid on his bed where he died shortly after, in his sleep, with the happiest expression on his face. What a fitting end to his fantastic career. May all your dogs leave so beautifully.

5
Breeding

I have lost count of the letters I have received which start 'Please tell me how I become an Afghan breeder?' My reaction nowadays is invariably the same, 'Why?'

Why do people wish to produce more puppies in an already overpopulated breed? From many conversations I have come to the conclusion that for a great many there are three prime factors: fortune, fame and glamour. However I can assure them that they are for the most part just delightful dreams – in which I suppose all of us have quietly indulged ourselves at some distant time.

As for fortunes, it should be realised that Afghan puppies grow so fast and need so much food, care and attention that they are not a sound economic proposition in terms of pure financial gain. The owner of one bitch with no great overheads may well find himself to be a little in pocket if he sells quickly and has managed to find a reasonably priced food supply.

If the breeders run a kennel, large or small, then they will be fortunate to break even, if they rear well and resist temptation to push the puppies out to a dealer or to the first buyer that appears, regardless of suitability. In the present economic climate not so many people can afford to buy a pedigree puppy, particularly one which in youth has a considerable appetite. Litters do not sell easily therefore. In fact it can be quite frightening to put in advert after advert and to find that the only responses are from people ringing up to see if you have any unwanted dogs free to a good home.

By the time they are four to five months old any profit will be nil and the food bill still increasing. At three months it will be necessary to inoculate them, in itself a considerable outlay.

Those who have only a small back garden and keep the puppies in the tool shed will be facing practical as well as financial difficulties and there is not always a fairy godmother to swoop down and remove them to pastures green.

Fame is won by only a few people in the Afghan world. Many people enter the world of dogs and show regularly with huge enthusiasm for a year or two. When, however, they have bred one or two litters and have achieved very little, possibly not even very good dogs then the gilt well and truly wears off the gingerbread and they vanish as quickly as they arrived.

Usually the only ones to achieve fame (and I doubt very much whether they would regard it in that light) are the long-term kennel owners who have passed through their long apprenticeship in showing, breeding and judging, who may be regarded as permanent and who have several generations of their kennelname in many pedigrees. Yet these may be people who now rarely breed unless they particularly want a new puppy for their own use or wish to prove a breeding point.

Glamour is most definitely in the eye of the beholder and not in the life of the average Afghan breeder. The onlooker sees only the handler and the dog sweeping into the ring in its immaculate show

BREEDING

coat. The handler may well be much more modestly dressed than the dog but undoubtedly on these occasions there is reflected glory which encompasses the owner, particularly if there is the glow of victory.

In reality breeders work hard, particularly if they own a kennel, cleaning out adults and puppies, preparing food, grooming, training and exercising, washing dishes, cleaning dirty runs, nursing sick dogs, fixing up injuries, and doing the thousand and one chores that can only occur where dogs are concerned, come hail, rain, or shine. It is sheer hard labour and can be a frantic worry.

Ch Ranjitsinjhi of Jagai owned by Mrs Jo Holden and bred by the author. 'Ranji', known as the 'Prince Charming of Afghans' was one of the most well known winners of his time, famous not only for his beauty but his enormous personality. Sired by Ch Waliwog of Carloway he was invariably shown in immaculate form and condition and won Best In Show at Richmond Champion Show in 1968. He is pictured here with his trophy as winner of the Hound Group at Crufts in 1969

BREEDING

Champions are bred it is true, but consider the number of Afghan champions in relation to the litters that are regularly produced – fantastically small. The dogs that gain their title have to be extraordinarily good to achieve this distinction and very few people, relatively speaking, manage to breed them.

It should also be remembered that it is largely the owner of the champion who is responsible for the status of his dog through his own determination and willingness to put aside his other interests for the express purpose of campaigning that dog.

It is rarely possible to thoroughly campaign more than one dog at a time; therefore, assuming that you have a superb litter and that you keep one, you will rely on others to show the dogs that you feel are also outstanding. Only if you are very lucky will you find someone buying your dog will have the tenacity of purpose, the strength of character to campaign that dog, to put up with the long distances that must be travelled to far-flung championship shows in all weathers and in all parts of the British Isles, to pay out enormous sums of money to cover petrol, food and accommodation in the process, to bear the disappointment of losing to lesser dogs, the setbacks, the long sessions of grooming and training.

I personally have bred many puppies, some I have thought brilliant, some good, many – to my shame – mediocre. Always I have tried to weed them out scrupulously. To people who have wanted to show I have always endeavoured to sell my best youngsters; to those that have only wanted a pet I have sold the others. Rarely have those good puppies been seen anywhere near a ring; the pets have appeared frequently, to my chagrin.

The overpopulation that I have mentioned is of course the direct result of the fact that so many jumped on the bandwagon to achieve one or all of those three factors when Afghans were in their heyday only a year or two ago. At that time anything sold and the 'get rich quick' merchants mated bitches at the drop of a hat to the nearest dog; they would go to a well known dog in order to gain the name of the breeding on the pedigree, but in no case did they bother to see whether the pedigrees linked kindly. There was no heed given to the unholy mixtures of conformation or temperament that were being perpetrated in the name of breeding. The result has been a great many poor Afghans, some barely recognisable as such, and alas it is still many of these which are being shown and used now. One hopes sincerely that in the future more attempts will be made to maintain a higher standard of both conformation, rearing and temperament instead of taking the easiest and cheapest course to the detriment of the breed.

If you do decide that, regardless of possible tragedies and discomforts, both financial, physical and mental, your whole present desire in life is to breed a litter, there are several factors that must be faced before you commence thinking in terms of stud dogs and brood bitches.

First of all where will your bitch whelp and where will you keep your puppies? It is quite impossible to keep baby Afghans in a flat without a garden, particularly if it is up several flights of stairs. Growing puppies can be messy and smelly little objects as well as lively and destructive, therefore they must have separate, easily cleaned accommodation and plenty of room for exercise.

Secondly will there always be someone there available in case of accidents such as a puppy strangling in its mother's coat, and to see that there are regular times for feeding, cleaning and exercising?

Thirdly, have you enough money put aside to rear a litter and to maintain your bitch really well? Nowadays, rearing to two months, plus the feeding of the bitch, stud fee, and veterinary attention could well cost more than £200 and as prices rise, probably much more. It is no use to think of possible future profits, the litter will need food and it will need it urgently.

Once the decision to breed has been taken it is necessary to consider the pedigree of your bitch dispassionately, if necessary with the aid of someone who knows the background of the dogs present in it. Try to find out what they looked like, whether they were large or small, heavy or finely boned, what sort of basic structure they had, if their temperaments were good and whether there were any hereditary faults in their background. Try to obtain pictures of forebears in order to check on all possible faults and virtues in accordance with the standard. Best of all, wherever possible try to see the parents of your bitch. Are they the types from which you would wish to breed?

Next, once more with expert help if necessary, look for an appropriate stud dog. There are several points to consider. In the first place, wherever possible follow a similar procedure to that which you followed with the pedigree of the bitch. In the next context one must think about its ancestry in relation to that of the bitch. Does it link up, does it completely duplicate itself or is it a complete outcross?

Now comes the question in related dogs of 'line breeding' and 'in-breeding'. Line breeding is not so closely interconnected as in-breeding. It will contain dogs of the same types and lines but it will not necessarily be the same animal that is used. For example, the grandsire of the dog may be a litter brother to an ancestor of the bitch. He may have been mated to the sister or mother of another of the forebears. In other words similar types may result but because the genes are disposed differently in litter brothers something fresh will be the logical outcome.

In-breeding is virtually duplication as in the example of a brother and sister mating or father–daughter alliance. Although you may be consciously in-breeding for type you are also doubling up on faults and weaknesses. Such matings should only take place after careful consideration of the temperament and hereditary factors and also only once in several generations.

Discussion with that eminent authority on eyes, Dr Keith Barnett of the Small Animals Centre at the Animal Health Trust, brought home the fact that the exaggeration of certain points for showing is very bad in principle. This matter arose when I showed him a partially blind seven-month old puppy with an overfine head and minute eyes who was proved to have congenital cataract as a result of breeding for a 'fine' show head. The stronger one from my own breeding, taken along as a check case, was pronounced as remarkably sound and a type which would not suffer from these faults. Dr Barnett quoted in particular the case of over-refined heads, the oddly shaped eyes found in some larger breeds such as St Bernards, and the problems caused by the sloping quarters of the Alsatian, and stated that the exaggerated show points we so often breed for leads to conditions and shapes that are physically and anatomically impossible.

If there is a complete outcross it may be a very good thing, provided the types match and there is no violent disparity, but do make sure that one is not taking a huge clod of a dog with a head like the proverbial bucket and then mating it to an overlong, lean wisp with a Borzoi head, no underjaw and claws for paws in the fond hope that the two together will cancel each other out and produce good puppies. It is very unlikely.

If, having faced all the facts, you realise that you do not know the first thing about it, get in touch with someone who does. You may think first of the breeder from whom you obtained your Afghan. If that is not possible contact your area Afghan club. If you do not know how to find someone to help, ring the Kennel Club. They will put you in touch with the nearest club secretary who will offer you advice and then put you in touch with someone nearer at hand who can offer you more concrete assistance. They will also advise you on where to obtain a suitable stud dog for your particular bitch.

Contact the owner of the stud dog in good time and discuss the bitch with him. They will usually be fairly honest as to whether your bitch and their dog will hit it off with regard to hereditary factors and few will press their stud dog to a wildly unsuitable bitch merely for the sake of a stud fee. After all, the resultant litter is still half their responsibility, shrug off the thought of bad puppies though they may.

Discuss the terms of use beforehand by finding out the dog's stud fee, and whether or not the owner would compromise on half the fee and a puppy; or, if you do not wish to spend money on a stud fee at all, would he insist on a pick of the litter or on the choice of two puppies. Remember that he is most likely to choose the best and you may have to face the heartbreak of seeing the puppy that you really like taken away. Make sure that you have all the arrangements settled well beforehand in the event of 'terms' instead of a fee – if possible in writing for even the nicest stud-dog owners can make mistakes or there can be misunderstandings. Most people give a receipt with the terms written upon it after mating, on payment of the stud fee. (The stud fee is paid after the mating has taken place but before the bitch goes home.) Usually a free return mating is guaranteed on the next season if the bitch does not conceive but this is not obligatory, it is purely a matter of goodwill on the part of the dog's owner. Remember the fee is for the actual service, not any resultant puppies.

In some cases the terms of breeding of the bitch will have been laid down while the bitch was still a puppy before actual purchase. The bitch could have been acquired under a loan-of-bitch agreement, whereby it could have been agreed before she changed hands that anything from a pick of the puppies to a whole first litter may have been spoken for by the bitch's breeder. It may even lay down the fact that the original breeder may have the right to arrange for the stud dog to be used. This transaction is usually entered upon an official Kennel Club form and each interested party has a copy while a third is lodged with the Kennel Club until such time as the contract is fulfilled.

It behoves everyone who is entering upon a contract of this nature to consider carefully what they feel is honest and acceptable. A breeder must try to acquire some return for labour but sometimes the conditions are downright iniquitous. Only recently I was surprised when someone brought their bitch down for approval to see if it matched up reasonably with my dog, that they handed me another piece of paper to look at with their pedigree. It stated that they were to give the first and second choice of their first litter to the bitch's breeder and was signed by both parties. I felt in my own mind that this was a little hard and that the breeder concerned could have asked for first and third choice and still have made a good profit, while leaving the owners at least one reasonably good puppy to show for their financial outlay and hard work. However I did not comment on that fact but merely said 'Oh, you did not pay for your puppy.' 'But', said they, 'we did' (quite a reasonable price as it turned out) 'but the breeder handed us this paper and said it was customary to sign this and we were so green that we did not realise what we were signing.' So do make sure that all is reasonable and do get advice beforehand if in doubt.

Let the owner of the dog know as soon as your bitch starts her season. He may ask you to bring it down a day or two before you estimate it will be ready for mating, in order that he may keep her under observation and so make sure that the mating takes place at exactly the right time, better both for her and her spouse. He may also allow her to stay for an extra day if she is excitable in order that she may have a second mating if this is felt to be necessary and in order to allow her to calm down and rest quietly after mating so that she will not be upset by a long journey immediately afterwards, with possible loss of puppies. This is extra kindness and helpfulness on the part of the dog's owner and although he has the best interests of your bitch at heart you must be prepared to pay for your bitch's keep during this period.

The season usually begins with a slight pinkish discharge which within a day or so becomes bloodstained. At the same time the vulva begins to swell and continues to do so for nearly two weeks, gradually softening until at about eleven to fourteen days it is completely soft, usually without any discharge. At this time the bitch will start to flip her tail sideways and the time is right for mating.

If your bitch has a male companion, he will make it very clear from his play and behaviour a week or two before you see signs of her season that her heat is due. Their keen sense of smell gives them advance warning. Bitches also tend to urinate frequently during this whole period as though leaving 'calling cards' for any passing dogs. Their scent is extremely strong and a bitch can cause quite a nuisance by attracting the male canine populace for some distance around. They camp outside the gate or find unsuspected methods of entry through neighbours' garages, gardens and fences. The only safe thing is to keep a bitch locked away indoors with no wide-open windows, and exercised behind a high unbroken fence so that marauders cannot enter and she cannot get out.

To test whether the bitch is ready for mating and the vulva really soft inside and out, gently insert a clean finger well coated with vaseline. If it can penetrate easily and meet no strictures then it is the right time for the mating to take place. The bitch at this time should, unless terrified by the antics of a large male, firmly stand her ground for him.

The time of eleven to fourteen days is only a rough average, since some bitches are ready for mating at the beginning of their season and others right at the end.

BREEDING

Remember that on no account should a bitch be mated until she she has reached the age of two years. This is written into the Afghan Hound Association Breeders Ethics and is most sound advice since Afghans are such slow-maturing creatures, and some bitches are barely mature at that age.

A dog may be tried out for stud as soon as he seems, to an informed opinion, sufficiently mature to perform efficiently. A potentially good young stud will spend quite a lot of his time indulging in sex play with both dogs and bitches and on no account should he be deterred from this in any harsh or unkind way that could spoil his career. Under no circumstances should he be made to feel that his behaviour is wrong, but if he becomes very trying he should be separated from the others for a while. Fortunately the violence of the young Afghan's sex urge gradually wanes and becomes normal.

Afghan dogs have been known to mate successfully at the age of ten or eleven months but usually they are best started around the age of fifteen months. Do not leave his first mating until he is about four years old however; the sooner he forms a romantic attachment the better.

If any stud dog is proven (has produced a litter), he can be legitimately presumed to be fertile and a full stud fee will be charged for him. If he is a maiden then it is usual to charge a token payment of half price or less, or to have a written agreement to take a puppy in lieu of stud fee if any are born.

It is never a good idea to mate two maiden Afghans since neither really knows what they are doing; the dog will be inexperienced, possibly oafish and probably fool about and the bitch may be physically and mentally hurt by his clumsy antics. It is surprising how much an experienced bitch can help a callow young dog whereas a frightened young female could hurt him and put him off for life. Therefore this factor must be taken into consideration when you choose your dog. Also, should you use a maiden dog on your maiden bitch, you will be unable to tell which animal was at fault in the event of an unfruitful mating and will not know what steps to take to remedy it.

On payment of the stud fee the pedigree should be forthcoming, together with the dog's Kennel Club registration number or stud book number. There can be no adequate reason why these should be withheld if the transaction has gone through, and also the pedigree should be readily available since it must have been there for examination before mating.

Once the mating is over nothing remains but to spend the next nine weeks exercising and feeding your bitch carefully and preparing for the happy event.

Ideally the period of gestation is sixty-three days but frequently puppies are several days early, and much less frequently, a few days late. Bitches can whelp normally any time after fifty-six days. If they are more than about three days late the vet should be consulted and, if necessary, a caesarian performed.

For the first four weeks after mating there is no visible change but at the end of that time the nipples will probably be slightly enlarged and gradually the girth of ribs and loins begins to increase.

Your vet will actually be able to give a prognostic diagnosis not earlier than twenty-one days after mating and not later than twenty-eight days.

Three or four weeks after mating you will probably find that your bitch becomes very finicky over her food and may occasionally vomit. After a few days the appetite usually returns with increased vigour and it is very probable that she has suffered from a similar tummy upset to that which affects so many human mothers-to-be. At the same time she may become extra demonstrative and start 'taking care of herself' by exercising a little less and not leaping about so much. A pregnant bitch getting off a chair is a much different sight from a carefree youngster.

There is, however, no hard-and-fast rule and some bitches will, in spite of strict supervision, insist on galloping around up to the last possible moment. Indeed bitches in the wild can keep on the move until far advanced in pregnancy. However, do regulate your expectant mother's exercise as carefully as possible and do not take her out too far in the last two weeks of pregnancy.

At five weeks the ribs start to barrel out slightly, then the loins, and the little whelps can be felt just below the ribs, rather like walnuts. By six weeks there is quite a considerable difference in size and weight and the puppies start to make their presence felt by kicking quite strongly. The movements increase in strength and frequency during the next three weeks.

As the weeks go by her daily intake of meat and vegetables should include good-quality red meat. Cheese, and biscuit and other starchy food should be reduced to avoid her being overweight. This can lead only to reduced muscle tone and subsequent lethargy when whelping. As her size increases it is better to give her daily ration of food in two or three smaller meals rather than in one large one for that causes discomfort. She should also have two good-quality milk feeds a day, either both of top-quality cow's or goat's milk or one of cow's milk and one of Lactol or Esbilac milk food. Goat's milk is particularly feeding if you are lucky enough to be able to obtain it.

By six weeks both the Canovel or Vetzyme and the vitamin capsule intake should have been doubled. It is essential that the vitamin capsule has an abundancy of vitamins C and D.

At this stage, fairly late in pregnancy, it is necessary to gather to-

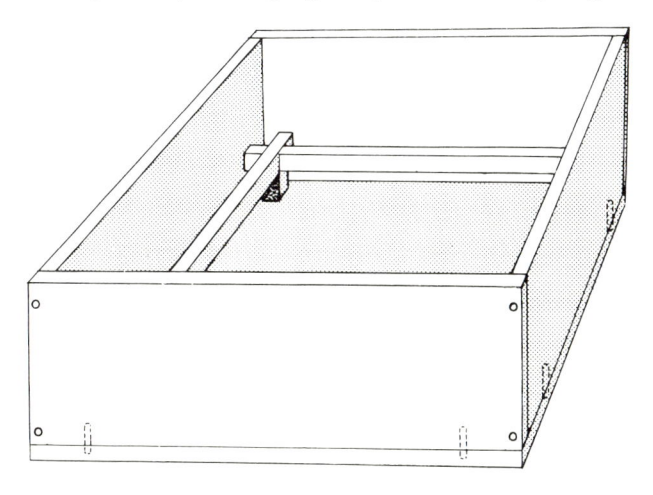

In this whelping box the sides are bolted at the floor and the corners for complete cleaning and easy storage. A simpler version can have permanent joints. The rail can be lifted out once the puppies are large enough to avoid being crushed

gether all the relevant equipment. However much you wish to economise, a well made whelping box is a necessity. An average size of box for an Afghan is about 3ft 6in square and the sides should be about 18in high. As they get very messy during whelping they must be easy to clean and I advocate one that comes to pieces so that no germs or minute detritus can be harboured in the cracks to cause trouble later on.

Mine is lined with plastic so that it can be easily wiped over with a disinfectant solution between the arrival of each puppy. The sides are screwed down to the base as well as being screwed together at the upright corners and it is remarkably easy to store flat, wrapped in polythene to keep it sterile, with the bolts attached in a bag (see illustration).

A guard rail which can be inserted into the box is a necessity, since it removes the possibility of a puppy being squashed between its mother and the side of the box. The rail need protrude only 4in from the side and the floor and can be made as a lift-out frame if the box is to be dismantled between litters.

The maternity bag should contain the following articles and should be left in a convenient place for ten days in advance of the labour date:

Strong thread.
Large lint squares, approximately 15in square.
Kitchen towel (large roll).
Antiseptic, Dettol, Savlon, or Lysol.
Petroleum jelly.
Scissors with rounded points.
Dropper.
Glucose.
Lactol, Esbilac, or fortified milk.
Brandy.

The scissors will be used for cutting the cord and possibly the sac enclosing the puppy and should be sharp but not so pointed that they can inadvertently damage a tender whelp.

Lint squares are invaluable for getting hold of slippery puppies, cleaning them and, if necessary, for producing a little soft friction.

The thread must be strong enough not to snap when a cord is being tied off and should also be just thick enough not to slip away from fingers that could well be rather messy.

The kitchen towel will be useful to catch afterbirths and for a general clean-up during these rather messy proceedings.

Petroleum jelly can be smeared just inside the vulva to ease and speed up the passage of the first puppy which can sometimes be lengthy and difficult with the tightly stretched skin and muscle.

Brandy can help your bitch if by any chance she does suffer from shock. A few drops only in warm milk can be very comforting. The dropper and glucose are for an emergency, such as a bitch without milk.

There are also very definite signs, quite unmistakeable at the beginning of the whelping period, one of which is an urgent desire to dig and scratch rapidly and thoroughly at carpets, flooring and furniture in the instinctive desire to prepare a bed for the offspring. If you have had the foresight to introduce your bitch to the box well beforehand, so that she enjoys sleeping in it, you may well be lucky enough for her to choose that patch to have her puppies and so escape damage.

Obviously from the foregoing it is necessary to choose the whelping site with great care. If you put aside a special kennel for this purpose, make sure that there is room for you to be there the whole time, providing yourself with the necessities for an overnight stay. Like most people I produce a mattress and lie relaxing but not sleeping beside the whelping box during the night and I find it is remarkable how a contented bitch with her puppies will try to insinuate her family and herself into your blanket with the sincere intention that we can be one happy family. Some are most determined on this score and puppies are shuttled from box to bed and back like tennis balls and almost as speedily.

If your bitch is going to whelp indoors, make sure that carpets and valuable furniture are removed – even the best trained bitch may have one or two accidents before or after whelping and this is the time for cossetting not scolding. You do not want to lose the seat of the settee during an unguarded moment.

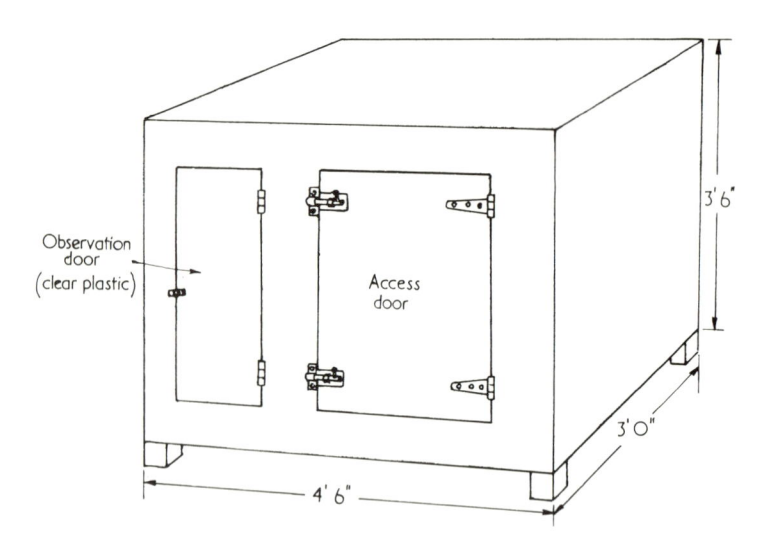

The framework of the insulated whelping box has internal and external skins of ply or oil-tempered hardboard. The cavities are filled with polystyrene sheets or glass fibre, easily dismantled for storage

See that the chosen place is draught-free and that there is adequate space to move around the whelping box. In an emergency, speed may decide between life and death. It should be moderately warm and well ventilated with facilities for hanging an infra-red lamp over the box. A door to the garden in case the bitch needs to make an emergency dash outside is a must, since even with the greatest care a bitch can become very loose.

The Animal Health Trust advocate a large 'lidded' whelping box. This contains bitch and puppies and uses body heat to keep them at an even temperature. The effect is rather like a huge doll's house and it is possible to have a polythene 'window' to enable the occupants to be examined without disturbances, while the mother can come and go through a curtained or normal doorway (see illustration). I saw this in use in Margaret Niblock's Khanabad kennels and her puppies were beautifully large, evenly balanced and obviously thriving. However, we both felt that there was a lack of the normal communication between bitch, puppies and owner, which is a feature of this kennel.

Have all your equipment ready and the whelping box in position a few days before the birth date, remembering that it could be early, then you are in a relaxed, business-like frame of mind once labour commences.

Most bitches refuse their last meal before signs of the proximity of whelping appear, but I can assure you that there are exceptions and you may well have one. I well recall one of mine eating a hearty evening meal very rapidly, so that I was quite sure that nothing would happen that night. Half an hour later I heard strange puppy squeaks and found her well and truly dug in to what can only be described as an inaccessible earthwork behind an ornamental fruit tree trained to a wall, with a shrieking puppy being systematically buried by her with its mouth full of earth. It was so thickly covered with soil on its damp little body that all I could do was wash it out under the tap. She obviously could not believe that it was anything to do with her and disclaimed it as a terrible mistake on her part all the way up to the house and into the whelping box, also regarding the next two arrivals as aberrations that a well bred bitch should ignore.

There are very definite physical signs that labour is due to begin. Several hours beforehand, even as much as forty-eight hours, the puppies begin to drop into position and there is a considerable increase in width round the loins. This unusual sensation often causes a great deal of fright in a maiden bitch and she whimpers a great deal. At this time she starts digging and scratching in order to prepare her bed. Her temperature will drop several degrees also, from the normal 101.3° F to 98° F.

Immediate signs of whelping are a swollen vulva and a rapid increase in the speed of breathing with intermittent bouts of 'talking' and a desire for comforting company. If a hand is placed just between the legs at the entrance to the birth channel it can be quite easily felt whether it is flat and empty or whether there is a hard bulge indicating that a puppy is in position ready to be born. At this time she starts to lick herself very urgently. As labour commences, the whining and talking stop and she concentrates on the matter in hand. At this point she stretches out in the box and the contractions can be seen moving down the body. It is interesting to note that the intense activity among the other puppies seems to calm down at this point, as though they are conserving their strength for the journey ahead.

The first puppy in its sac of water appears like a large black bubble at the opening vulva and the bitch pushes in earnest. Sometimes it appears and disappears if the contractions are not sufficiently strong, but finally it is expelled. A word of warning to novices: a maiden bitch may well give a nerve-shattering scream at this point as membranes are stretched. The pain is very quickly over and forgotten, however, as she starts to lick her puppy.

The puppy finally appears in a rush in a messy brownish puddle, usually enclosed in its sac and still attached by the cord. If the mother does not immediately start to rip open the sac to clean the puppy you must do this for her, quickly.

First gently pierce the sac and remove it from the puppy to clear it away from the surrounding water, or it will drown. Be careful while doing this that you do not pull on the cord and cause an umbilical hernia. If it does not cry or breathe, turn it upside down so that water may run out of its nose and mouth and gently but firmly rub its body with your hands, or the lint, and in stubborn cases give a gentle pressure on the ribs as in artificial respiration. This will expel inhaled water and usually start it functioning properly. Then, when you are satisfied that it can breathe properly, tie a piece of thread firmly round the cord about 1in away from the body just beyond the very slight thickening of the umbilical cord as it leaves the stomach. This must be tied very tightly as it restricts any flow of blood from the body when the cord is cut beyond the knot (away from the puppy) to free it from the afterbirth. During all this there may be a few difficulties in the shape of a wriggling slippery little body while you are trying to tie your knot, and a mother frantic to see what you are doing to her offspring.

The next step is to clear away the mess and see that the afterbirth to which the whelp was attached is safely removed. This is often ejected at the same time as the puppy but it sometimes comes away a few minutes later. It is essential to check that each one is produced, since an afterbirth that is retained can cause trouble and even death.

Most bitches do all the work themselves but in the case of a large litter they can tire and you may, once more, have to help. In the case of a puppy being wedged while presented and visible, grasp it carefully but firmly by inserting the thumb and forefingers into the vagina and gently ease it out as the bitch strains down. On no account should you pull at other times and never grasp the head and pull. Usually if the head is presented first, and the puppy is large or the canal tight, the sac breaks and the puppy may be breathing before birth. It is even more dangerous if the puppy's legs appear without the membrane enclosing it. On each occasion it should be withdrawn as speedily as possible. Soapy lather on the hand often makes the insertions of the fingers easier.

If the bitch strains for an hour or more without success, or if she is too worn out with a large litter to cope easily, contact your vet immediately. He can give injections to speed birth easily and harmlessly, or he may advise a caesarian to counteract the lack of oxygen to the unborn whelps. Do take his advice. Do not risk a bitch's life for the sake of economy as I have known people to do.

Some vets do not wish to travel out of their town surgeries nowadays but no more harm will come to a bitch by popping her into the car and taking her to the surgery than will occur by leaving her. In fact, it is surprising how often one can find that the obstinate little object that has caused all the trouble through failing to appear is happily suckling from mother when you park the car at the surgery.

Few people would advocate that a bitch should eat all the afterbirths, although it is natural in the wild and gives the mother a sustaining warm meal after her labours.

A few breeders allow her to eat just one to clear her bowels after all the upset and strain. The fact remains that they can cause the bitch to be quite violently loose in her motions and I always try to intercept them.

Birth is a most messy process and during its seemingly endless progress the box is going to need constant washing with a reliable disinfectant and constant relining with newspaper to keep it sweet and clean before the next arrival. Hoard clean newspaper like gold dust therefore.

During whelping and afterwards it is necessary to have a little nest available in which to place the puppies while another is arriving or the mother receives attention. A cardboard box with high sides, containing a warm hot-water bottle covered with a blanket so that the box interior is kept at blood heat, is invaluable.

Between births, she will lick and cuddle her babes who will take their first feed of colostrum, but frequently no real feeding takes place until the last one has arrived. One of the most delightful sounds I know comes from the whelping box: the gentle crooning of a busy, happy bitch and the contented murmuring from her offspring.

Once all the puppies have safely arrived the bitch should be led out to relieve herself (during the first two or three times this happens see that no unsuspected small late arrival is dropped on the ground and left unheeded). During this period the box can be thoroughly cleaned and disinfected and the puppies checked over for any obvious physical abnormalities such as missing paws or tails or twisted legs. If any are found they must be put to sleep, but on no account should you do this yourself since you could cause pain even to one so small. Leave the wreckling with the others and give it to your vet to deal with when he checks the bitch. Done professionally, death is sure, swift and painless.

When the bitch returns from outside, she should be cleaned up around the hindquarters with an antiseptic, soapy solution. This will be absolutely necessary, since they will be soaked and encrusted in the messy discharge from the vagina which, if left, will turn greenish and smell evilly, as well as being most unhygienic.

She will need regular sponging and drying, because there will be a slight but steady oozing for several days until all is healed inside.

Your vet should check the bitch over for any signs of an unborn puppy or the retention of an afterbirth and will in all probability give an antibiotic injection to prevent infection and speed rapid internal healing.

Once having whelped, the bitch will need considerable quantities of milk to enable her to keep a plentiful supply of milk flowing for her puppies. During the whelping she can also be fortified by drinks of warm milk and glucose, but obviously she will not require solid food at this time. Vitamins and the calcium supplement must be given regularly, not only for the puppies' sake but for hers; lack of calcium in her diet could lead to eclampsia which causes milk fever and fits and can, at that stage, be dealt with only by your vet.

For about thirty-six hours after whelping it is advisable to keep her on a fairly light but feeding diet. Milk meals, including porridge with eggs and glucose beaten in, are very soothing to a tummy that may be slightly upset, particularly if she has managed to eat a lot of afterbirths. For the first few hours omelettes, flavoured with cheese or onions, will be an essentially satisfying food and then she can graduate to a few meals of fish and from then on back to good red meat.

If the litter is very large it may be advisable to supplement their feeding with one or two hand-fed meals a day. There may also be the disaster of the bitch lost during whelping or the bitch unable to produce milk in spite of veterinary help. These are three mishaps that can happen to any breeder, experienced or a newcomer to the business.

The most successful substitute is that miracle, a foster mother, of any breed whatever – it does not matter how mixed her parentage! This, with luck, may be standing by through the good offices of a vet, a breed club or through frantic telephone calls to all the kennels around. Puppies do not care if mother suddenly turns into a basset hound or a poodle as long as the milk is there. I have had a most mournful basset foster mother who insisted on sleeping in my bed to keep her happy (I would have put up with anything to save my puppies). The second foster I used was a minute miniature poodle – hardly larger than the pups – and possibly the most successful was an adorable black-and-white mongrel who brought her three fat babies with her and whom we reared alongside my splendidly bred orphans.

The next emergency alternative is to use a minute feeding bottle such as a premature baby bottle or a puppy feeder, or, as an alternative for a very weak puppy, a dropper. The two former are the most successful if the puppy will accept an artificial teat and most will suck away happily with little risk of it going down the wrong way. It is necessary to enlarge the hole of the teat for puppies' use by piercing it with a hot needle.

The dropper is useful for very weak or unco-operative puppies but holds definite hazards. Milk can be inserted into the mouth and go down the air passage into the lungs, inevitably causing pneumonia and the probable death of the puppy. Great care must therefore be taken to see that the dropper is well and truly inserted into the mouth so that the puppy uses its tongue and soft palate as it would on a bitch's teat. The sucking action takes place quite far back in the mouth compared to a human's use of the lip.

The third form of feeding, and this I must emphasise can only be undertaken with the guidance and help of an expert, and not as an academic exercise in puppy rearing, is by use of a catheter. This is commonly referred to as tube feeding. Introduce a long, flexible tube with a finely tapered polished end, straight from the mouth, down the oesophagus, to the stomach, thus by-passing the windpipe. This tube is attached to the barrel of a hypodermic which contains the correct quantity of milk. Before filling, the tube is measured against the length from the puppy's mouth to the stomach, the equivalent being marked on the length of tubing from the point for insertion upwards. The correct amount of milk feed is then drawn up into the tube and so to the hypodermic, and all air bubbles must be carefully eliminated. The tube is gently inserted over the tongue and eased down the throat, helped by the puppy's natural swallowing action, being immediately withdrawn if it meets any obstacle and the whole process is started again. Gradually it is inserted into the stomach with the head held fairly well back on the neck to ensure a clear easy passage, until the mark on the tube meets the lips. At this point the liquid is gently expelled into the stomach and the tube withdrawn. Obviously a handler is needed for the puppy.

With any of these methods the first four or five days will require a routine of two-hourly feeding day and night. An alarm clock and vacuum flask of puppy food are invaluable aids.

If for some reason the bitch cannot look after her offspring herself, you must replace her attentions. They must be regularly cleaned and their bowels stimulated. Damp cotton wool should be used in the same way as the bitch's tongue, to gently but firmly wipe over the rectum and anus to wipe away urine and faeces and to cause further excretion. More damp cotton wool should be used to wipe over the rest of the body and face since this both cleans and soothes the puppy. Any urine left on the stomach or in the groin will cause painful and messy burns to its skin.

Considerable patience and fortitude are necessary to achieve a successful outcome for a litter.

There is considerable controversy among breeders as to the advisability of culling a large litter. Some breeders will keep only six, others eight and some will keep all. The theory behind this is that a bitch can do a certain amount well; for a larger quantity standards may suffer. When culling takes place, size and health are taken into account as also are the advantages of one sex or colour as opposed to another, saleswise.

I do not agree with culling and have never practised it. By one's own insistence that a bitch has been mated one has, in some small measure, and however unthinkingly, tried to play God, and have responsibly brought life into the world. It seems to me that it is utterly irresponsible to reverse the process because the quantity does not fit your own plans neatly. As a result I struggle on night after night making sure that all my large litters have supplementary feeding whenever necessary.

Never attempt to mate your bitch too late in life. If by the time she is passing four, she has not already had a litter, it is risky to think of breeding from her, and by the age of six a maiden bitch is a most insecure proposition. The pelvic bones will have begun to stiffen, the birth passage will be tighter and she will no longer, however healthy, have the resilience and stamina of youth. From bitter experience I would never advise delaying a litter from a bitch that you wish to use, in order not to interfere with her show career. If she is so good she will successfully take up again from where she left off. Have a litter as soon after the age of two as possible and she will then be able to produce a litter after her career is ended with no ill effects. Although I am made well aware that

American, Canadian and Portuguese Ch Gini's E. Magnus Rex of Foxrun. Owned by one of the few Afghan enthusiasts in Portugal, Miss Carla Molinari of the Vale Negro Kennel, 'Rex' is an American bred dog from the Stormhill kennel

people have successfully had a first litter from a bitch of six or seven, in view of the well publicised tragedies that have occurred I now feel that to do so is irresponsible.

You should also give careful thought to the time of year in which your litter will arrive. If a bitch is mated in early October you will be spending your Christmas Day serving five meals a day to small hungry puppies, instead of enjoying your holiday. You will also experience the difficulties of rearing a litter which cannot go outside in bad weather and which will cause your electricity and fuel bills to rise drastically.

Finally, do realise that you will only get back what you have put in. This applies at all times, but it applies in particular to the quality of treatment received by the in-whelp bitch.

Still on the subject of quality, it may be helpful to realise that if you become established in the breed and start to produce a successful line you will, sooner or later, be asked to export a dog, and it must be clearly understood that only the best should go abroad since they represent British stock. They will be widely campaigned, will represent a considerable outlay on the purchasers' part and will be looked upon as a breeding or stud investment.

All too often the best remains at home, the reason being given that no-one has such good dogs as the British and that second best will reach the required standard. This is nonsense; there are superb dogs abroad.

The Americans produce fabulous specimens, although rather different in concept from ours with more bias towards showmanship. They trust that only the absolute cream will be sent there. Then the Scandinavians own dogs with American and British bloodlines which are second to none. The Continental breeders, in particular the Germans and Belgians, usually like to pick their own dogs: they are most knowledgeable and will always choose the most outstanding Afghan possible. France too has dogs of several lines and demands well tried stable lines. Exports for Spain and Italy must be carefully chosen to blend with the American and Scandinavian bloodlines to be found there. Australians also welcome top class stock and are critical of anything they feel does not reach the required standard.

BREEDING

When approached by a prospective buyer send a representative set of pictures of your dog, standing, side view and front, and a head study, together with a copy of the pedigree, the price of the dog ex-kennel, and a list of the costs involved so that the purchaser is in no doubt about the total outlay. Costs include the Kennel Club export pedigree, health certificate, any relevant blood tests and vaccinations, travelling crate, insurance and travelling expenses. It is usual to receive all the monies involved before the dog leaves the country.

In order to obtain details about the export of dogs to various countries you should contact the Ministry of Agriculture, Fisheries and Food, Animal Health Division, Hook Rise, Tolworth, Surbiton, Surrey. They will send, by return, a statement of all regulations regarding export to the stated country, necessary forms and time limits for health certificates. The other person to contact is your local veterinary surgeon, appointed by the Ministry to deal with any official health certificates and inoculations.

If you feel that you cannot deal with all the involved business yourself there are many excellent and old-established firms such as Ryslip who will undertake the whole job for you, including the paperwork, producing the correct size of travel box and delivery of the dog at the airport. In the case of a complicated business like an export to Australia I would recommend that you definitely use their services.

6
Puppy Rearing

Regardless of its aesthetic quality, the health, condition and future well-being of your puppy, whether you have bought it or reared it yourself, will depend upon its feeding, not only from weaning but also from many weeks before its birth.

Naturally only a healthy bitch, in the peak of condition, should be bred from, but she will still need to receive that little bit of extra attention soon after mating.

A multivitamin capsule daily with a general conditioner such as Linetone, Canovel Vetzyme or S.A. 37 will get her over her season and into sparkling condition and for the next three weeks she will not need any drastic extras, just a sensible diet with good fresh meat and roughage. During this period she should be checked regularly for any sign of an unusual discharge from the vulva, or any appearance of being run down or out of condition. Do not at this time try to economise on veterinary attention if you think it may be necessary.

After three weeks she should be given a daily dose of a calcium supplement in the form of steamed (sterilised) bone flour or the appropriate calcium tablets such as di-calcium phosphate. A daily pint of milk and an egg will give a food supplement for the developing whelps without causing excessive fat and she must be given regular steady exercise in order to keep the muscles firm for the hard work ahead.

Once the bitch has whelped, the onus for feeding the puppies is entirely on her since their sustenance entirely derives from her milk. Therefore it is most important that the excellent feeding provided for her before the birth continues after the arrival of the litter. She will need several pints of milk each day in order to keep a really plentiful supply flowing all the time. It must be born in mind that she could produce anything from eight to twelve puppies, and that they will be feeding nearly continuously, day and night. In order to continue with the pattern of sturdy bone growth that will have started before their birth, it is also essential that the dam has a suitable quantity of sterilised bone flour in her own food, at least one tablespoonful mixed in each meat meal. She will also need to continue with the double ration of vitamins for at least as long as she is continuing to feed them at all.

Food will at this time assume monstrous proportions in her mind since she needs it, not only to keep up her own strength which is being severely taxed, but also to help provide sustenance for her surprisingly active brood. Consequently she must be supplied with probably two, or even more, pounds of meat daily plus all her supplements and any vegetable that she may feel inclined to eat.

A graph of each puppy's weight and growth rate will give an excellent idea of the progress of your litter (see illustration). This should be started on the day of their birth with a recording of the

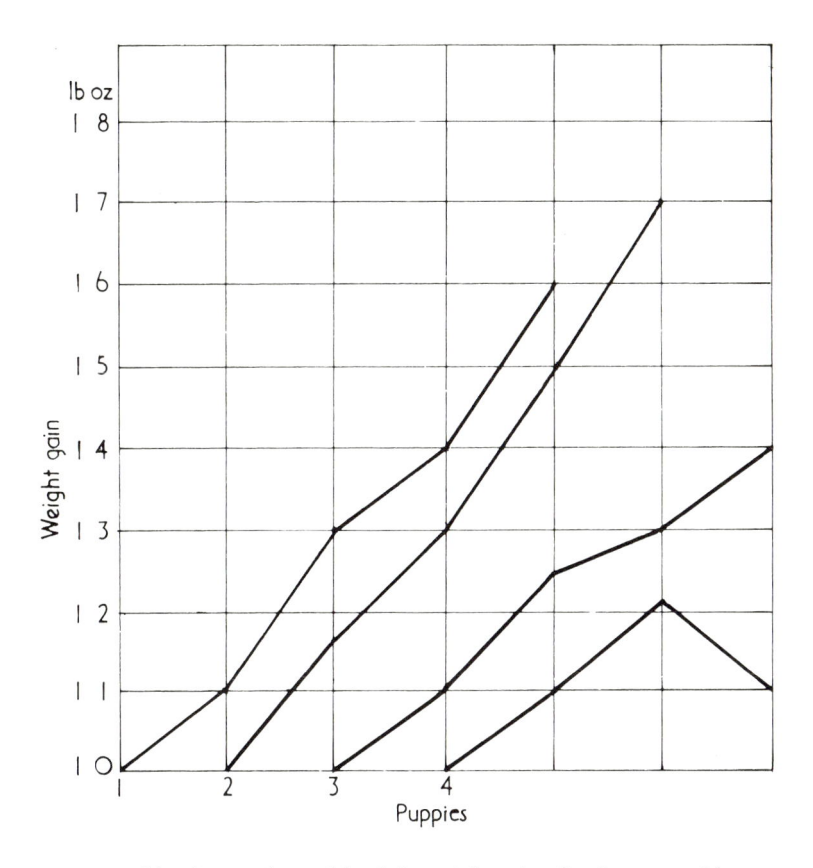

It is useful to keep a chart of the daily weight gain of each puppy, either separately or collectively. This one shows a steady weight increase for three puppies but number four is in trouble

birth weight of each puppy and then each one should have its progress recorded daily. That way you can check that growth is even, that there is not one puppy lagging behind the others and it also provides an opportunity to look each one over regularly so that any problems in bone, skin or general development will be promptly discovered.

Some people find identification a dreadful problem. In some litters there is no difficulty since there are obvious differences and a typical set of descriptions would be as follows.

Black dog.
Black dog, white forepaws.
Black dog, white right forepaw.
Black dog, white hindpaws.
Golden bitch, black mask.
Golden bitch, self mask.

But when they are all extremely similar — for example, all golden self masks — then other means of identification must be found. One method is to draw maps of the lighter patches almost invariably found on the 'shirt fronts' from the throat to the other end of the ribs. Another is to use a non-glossy lipstick on the soft skin of their tummies. The chart then reads according to the marks.

From the age of two weeks onwards the puppies' eyes will gradually start to open and this is the signal to start supplementary feeding and weaning. First they must be gently taught to lap and, although they may seem to be small unthinking creatures, they must not be forced to put their noses in milk in a most terrifying manner since instincts for fear or pleasure are already with them. I always take each puppy separately on my lap (well covered in towelling) so that he feels close and secure, and offer it milk in a tablespoon. This is much more in proportion to a puppy's size than the vast shiny expanse of a saucer into which it is demanded that it puts its nose. Some grasp the idea of putting their head toward the milk without any further coaxing but others need to have the idea brought home by having a finger, dipped in milk, inserted into their mouth to suck. If, after a few repeats of this, it still cannot realise what the spoonful of milk is for, do not worry, it is obviously just a little slower than some of its brothers and sisters and will be able to hold its own with the spoon of milk in a day or so.

Once the puppy has realised that this is an enjoyable and satisfying experience it can graduate to a larger dish of milk alongside the rest of the litter which will help to instil confidence into the most retiring small creature. The first feeds en masse will undoubtedly be a most messy experience since the puppies will put not only their noses but also their heads, ears and all their feet into the milk and also tend to wander backwards and forwards in the dish, with an occasional collapse into it. After they have finished, give them back to their mother who will practically gain another milk feed just by cleaning them up.

Once the puppies are able to take milk on their own, their growth rate will increase by leaps and bounds since they will also at this stage still be taking milk from their mother as well. In effect they will be receiving double rations. Once they can adequately use their mouths (after only a few feeds from a dish), a baby cereal can be added to make the consistency more solid and also a few drops of Abidec, cod liver or halibut liver oil can be added, well stirred into the feed to ensure that each puppy somehow manages to assimilate the required amount necessary for his daily growth.

Although it is natural to wish one's puppies to grow large and strong as quickly as possible, do not allow them to become seriously overweight. This is just as bad for them as being undernourished and can be damaging to bones and joints in a relatively unformed state.

Within a day or so a more savoury meal may be introduced in the form of a nourishing beef broth with wholemeal bread crumbled into it and with finely scraped beef which can be easily dealt with by tiny jaws whose teeth are only just appearing. The beef should literally be scraped since, at this early stage, even minced beef would be too coarse but, within a few days, they are well capable of consuming fine minced beef with small pieces of lightly crisped wholemeal bread for roughage. Although there are a great many adverts for puppy meals specially ground to pinhead size for small jaws, there is nothing in the commercial dog-biscuit line that contains the same food value as good wholemeal bread made from top-quality flour, and, if it is crisped up like a rusk in the oven, it has just as many beneficial results on the jaw as a commercial biscuit.

By the age of four weeks they should be taking a breakfast of porridge or baby cereal with an egg, in the proportion of half an egg per puppy beaten in with about half a teaspoonful of glucose, or honey, for each mouth. The sweeteners are not just to make it more palatable but to provide the natural, easily assimilated forms of sugar to replace the energy burned up by an active puppy. My own personal preference for the first daily meal is for a very nutritious, feeding, dish of porridge to which I also add, as well as the eggs and honey, really creamy milk and their vitamin drops. It makes a solid fuel to start the day and the puppies love it after the night's fasting (or semi-fasting according to the maternal instincts of the bitch).

If you decide to use cod-liver oil, or halibut-liver oil, you must not give the vitamin capsule, and any dosage of either of these oils must be very carefully regulated since they are very strong indeed and can have the opposite effect from that desired, if administered in too large a quantity, taking the calcium out of the bones and giving it to the kidney and muscle. Too enthusiastic application will undo all the good work.

There are mixed feelings about the advisability of giving the whole egg in the food. Some vets advise feeding the yolk only, because of the Avidin contained in the egg white. This has the property of destroying the Biotin in the intestine; however, since this process is cancelled out by a yeast product such as Canovel or Vetzyme it seems to be an unnecessary worry.

At five weeks the puppies should be established with a routine of five meals a day, which includes two meat meals, one at midday and the other in the early evening. The meat meal should consist of good quality beef, cooked or raw, giving approximately 2oz to each puppy with baked bread or terrier-sized meal mixed in to it. Sterilized bone flour must be added to both these meals at the rate of about one half teaspoonful to each puppy at each meal. A commercial supplement such as di-calcium phosphate can also be recommended, since the dosage is worked out ready for administration to either adults or puppies. The flavour of these supplements does not always appeal to dogs and therefore it is always a good idea to mix it well into a highly flavoured gravy with onion or garlic as an addition. If the litter will eat them it is an excellent plan to add chopped vegetables to the food and the gravy can usefully be made by using the vegetable juice. The more natural minerals that can be given to the puppy the better.

By six weeks the puppy should be well able to feed himself and be a self-sufficient little entity, fully weaned and able to live without his mother. But they are not ready for sale at this age.

At eight weeks onwards it may be possible to cut out one of their milk feeds, either the one at 4 pm or at bedtime. However I do not advise skimping just to avoid the inconvenience of having one's time so rigidly taken over, therefore I would advise keeping them on as many meals as possible for as long as possible.

The puppies will still at this age have breakfast, a meal which can usefully be continued as long as possible. Most start to quietly ignore it from about nine weeks on, usually when they leave home and start to feel more grown up. This is, of course, somewhat embarrassing when each puppy leaving with its new owner has 'breakfast' firmly written on its diet sheet and then obstinately refuses to contemplate it next morning. There are usually anxious 'phone calls which vary from a worried 'Is he ill?' to a suspicious note creeping in, indicating that you never really fed breakfast at all – this was obviously just window dressing so that you could charge a higher price and boast what a well reared puppy you were selling. Let me add, however, that some of the greedier ones will take breakfast all their lives and sometimes have to have it stopped deliberately because of threatening obesity.

If your puppy resolutely forsakes the habit of a morning meal then offer it egg, milk and glucose after it has been galloping around for about an hour and this will ensure that it has an appetite for some nourishing refreshment even if it turns up its nose at porridge as being a baby food.

Generally speaking it should for its milk feeds have milk and glucose but for its 4 pm one it could take a fortified baby food. A drink of milk at bedtime, a little while before it is put out to relieve itself, is a good idea but do give it time for the drink to settle before bedtime and so eliminate the risk of puddles. This risk of course is not so dreadful in the case of the puppy that is still actually in the kennel and I for one would rather mop up those puddles and know that my puppy was adequately fortified for the night than leave out that last feed.

Daily each puppy, whether in a home or the kennel, must continue to have a vitamin supplement which he can now take in capsule form. The sooner he can be put on to swallowing these the

Ch Horningsea Tiger's Eye with his little daughter who became Ch Horningsea Tiger Doll. An excellent example of really good rearing, the coat shows a good texture, the bone structure is really sound, the eyes clear and the attitude really alert and confident (Silvia Duran)

better, for it ensures that he receives his fair share. He must also have a daily ration of conditioner, which can be given in tablet form, using the same conditioners as before. Most will eat them from your hand or when put into the feeding bowls. Gradually, as the puppies grow, they are increased in quantity, the norm being one tablet for each 10lb weight of dog.

Naturally meat, milk and roughage are increased to feed a growing body and by three months he will be eating a really enormous quantity of meat – sometimes up to 2lb a day. However, his whole eating pattern eventually changes and he gradually takes himself off his midday meal by starting to nibble at it in a half-hearted manner and then finally ignoring it altogether. By early evening he will be ravenous and demanding a large evening meal, probably with 'afters' if he can get it. So $1\frac{1}{2}$lb will disappear as if by magic, but when his growth has stabilised and he starts to fill out at around ten months to a year, he will probably eat far less without histrionics and intimations that he is a poor, starving pup.

He still needs his bone flour until a year old and should continue to have it if you feel that he is a slow developer and is still growing, however slowly. The conditioner should continue all his life.

There are many proprietary dog foods produced by various firms such as Science Diet, Purina dog Chow, Spratts All in One. Contents are scientifically balanced and are extensively tested. They are produced by reputable manufacturers and have the added advantage of being very easy to feed. I was a guest in an American household where four dogs were kept in beautiful condition and feeding arrangements took only 5min daily, since each dog had a carefully measured bowl of Science Diet and water and there was no messy slicing up of meat and mixing with gravy. The dogs were very happy with it but all the time, while envying the ease with which feeding was accomplished, I knew in my heart that my own dogs would have given the mixture an icy and reproachful stare and utterly refused even to contemplate it since they enjoy chewing a chunk of meat so much. Many breeders feel as I do that every dog which runs fairly wild in large compounds – often more than an acre in area – needs a basic diet of fresh meat, and if a proprietory brand is used the dogs usually prefer to have some meat added and here there is a snag, particularly in the hot summer months, since most of these foods are meant to be eaten over a period of time with water available, and meat attracts flies.

Manufacturers give a complete breakdown of their contents and recommend that it is not necessary to give dietary supplements such as calcium. I am aware that this is correct but somehow always have that feeling that I should give more – just to make sure. I gather that I am not alone in this.

Tinned food is not for rearing little ones. Analysis proves they have a high moisture content and less food value. Indeed, having seen the quality of meat bought at slaughterhouses by some manufacturers, I am strengthened in my conviction that nothing pays in the long run like old-fashioned red meat.

However good the food that you feed your puppies and however large the quantity, nothing will do them much good if there is worm infestation and a large portion of their intake is cannibalised before it has a chance to give any benefit whatsoever.

At three weeks each puppy must be wormed, regardless of whether or not there is any visible proof of their presence. However carefully a bitch was wormed and looked after, larval worms are released at birth and pass through the womb into the pup and no one can be sure that their puppies are clear. Tablets can be obtained from your vet. They are very simply administered, either crushed in milk or popped straight down the throat. The puppies must be carefully watched to make sure that the tablets are not regurgitated and it is essential to have a fool-proof system of separating them and identifying them so that no one receives two doses or, worse, none at all. No long period of starvation is required but the dose is usually followed by a drink of warm milk or a light snack after a half-hour interval. After two weeks a second worming session must follow, and then every two weeks until four months. After that they should be wormed each month until the bitches are eight months and the dogs twelve months. After this, once you are really convinced that your dog is worm-free, the process should be repeated at six-monthly intervals to ensure that food always gives maximum benefit and you will be assured of the best possible results for your efforts.

Make sure during this vital year that the puppy has at least a pint of milk daily and more will not come amiss, provided that he is not constitutionally a 'fatty'. During this growth period every puppy should, on a reasonable diet, have steady bone growth with no problem of rickets, a fair covering of flesh over the bones without obesity, and excellent health throughout.

7
Showing

What fun showing can be, providing that you do not take it too seriously so that all your enjoyment is spoilt by a few losses, and it becomes a cut-throat, grim-faced, snarl-at-the-judge business.

If you decide that your puppy is of sufficient calibre to show well, then he will require a session of ring training daily from about four moths onward.

In England no puppy can be shown until six months old, when it is eligible for minor puppy classes, and indeed so slow is the development, both physical and mental, of some puppies that they seem too young to be involved in such a serious business. The minor puppy class is for dogs from six to nine months and the puppy class for dogs from six to twelve months. As you will realise, there is great variation between those of six months, just out for the first time, and a more mature, heavier coated youngster of twelve months. Nevertheless, do not despair, it is quality that counts.

In the United States there are classes for babes of two months onwards, when they are trained to show with the utmost self-possession and learn to be 'stacked' just like their older relatives. It is a most charming sight to see these puppies toddling seriously round the ring, but by the time they would only be making their delightfully fresh debut into the show ring here, they are already seasoned campaigners, with all the self-possession and ring craft in the world. Puppy classes at the American specialities are not as amusing or chaotic as here when young Afghans are on display for the first time in their lives, and find it a traumatic or hilarious experience – according to their temperament.

Training must be taken seriously, although naturally you want your puppy to enjoy it to the full, since a happy dog shows far better than a miserable one.

Since, no matter how beautiful your dog looks when he stands, movement is of prime importance to the judge, it is, above all, necessary to have your dog moving easily and freely on the lead. If your dog is sound, he will, given the opportunity, move equally soundly. If he is unsound or badly constructed in any way, then, once he is moved from the stacked position he will 'fall apart' and the good judge will undoubtedly penalise him. This means that to show his worth he must move on a loose lead with head well raised since he is a gazehound and not a 'sniff' hound following a scent. (This latter propensity unfortunately can occur to the most beautifully presented hound if a bitch in season has preceded him into the ring, but a dab of perfume on his nose end might disguise the scent).

Hold your dog on a loose lead and trot or run briskly so that his front legs extend well before him in a long, reaching stride, and his hindlegs show a strong thrusting drive that propels him forward. Do not allow him to prance with paws high in the air like a trotting horse since this means one of two things: either he has an abominably straight shoulder or you are taking him so slowly that he cannot reach out without leaving you, nor can he move comfortably. For training, the inevitable titbit held forwards and upwards until the head is at a keen angle is invaluable. Practise turning smartly at a right angle with the dog moving alongside you because the judge will not wish to wait while you sort out the confusion of a lead tangled round you and the dog as you turn in the ring. Such a pause can also spoil the sequence of your dog's movement when he is well into his stride. Sometimes, when a dog settles into a really lovely steady movement, you may find that the judge will ask you to move again without stopping just because it is giving the dog such an excellent chance and sometimes (I have been guilty of this once or twice) because he looks so beautiful on the move that they are just enjoying the picture. I once in fact was so enthralled when judging a specials class in America by the sight of a huge group of champions moving with their impressive, stylish movement that I quite forgot to stop them, and almost had some exhibitors in a state of collapse.

The next stage in training your dog to show is to train him to stand. They are placed in the ring usually facing in an anti-clockwise direction and therefore your dog's left side is his show side. There are rare occasions when you may feel it necessary to turn your dog in the opposite direction and there is no hard-and-fast rule about this, just custom. This can be done when the dog is standing 'in a hole' so that his stance is not correct, or when he insists on interfering with the dog in front. If you do turn your dog, however, you must see that the dog and exhibitor behind you are not distracted.

He must be trained to stand still for lengthy periods of several minutes at a time, so that a judge can go round the ring assessing possibly sixty dogs, and so that he can, at any time, see yours, standing in position. His head should be poised comfortably but high and proudly on a neck held firm and straight. His front legs should be well under the shoulder, not stretched forward. To achieve this, if your dog does not put himself naturally in position, put your hand between his front legs, lift him slightly and let his feet drop to the ground. They will assume the stance correct to his own frontal conformation. Do not be tempted to train your dog to stand overstretched. His hindquarters have a natural stance and it is useless to stretch back the upper thigh from the hip to give an obtuse angle. It will not give more angulation to the stifle, merely give a remarkably unsound appearance to the hip joint and cause a sagging top line, and either make the dog put his front paws forward to balance or cause him to put them back to straighten himself. I know that some expert handlers are able to manage this stretching and surreptitiously prop up their charges by a judiciously placed knee in the middle, but here startling glamour is being put before soundness, which is not conducive to ultimate high standards in the breed.

The judge will need to examine your dog's mouth to check on the bite and dentition. Train your puppy from the start to have his mouth handled. Do this by keeping the teeth closed and gently opening the lips so that it is quite apparent that he has a scissor or level bite, and so that it can be seen whether he has all his premolars. This is obligatory on the Continent and more and more of our own judges make a check when they have time in our huge breed classes.

Some owners prefer to show the judge the bite themselves but a good judge likes to make very sure about the teeth for himself, for experienced and cunning handlers can hide any amount of faults. If a dog has a good temperament it should not object to all this handling and if its temperament is not adequate then you should not consider showing it anyway.

In England only the quality of the bite is inspected and the breed standard merely states that there should be a scissor or level bite. No mention is made of the necessity for full dentition or otherwise. In Scandinavian and Continental countries full dentition is demanded and dogs without a full set of teeth are penalised, therefore each judge makes a detailed inspection to see that the pre-

Ch Shangrila Pharahna Phaedra, a truly superb bitch belonging to Dr Gerda Maria Kennedy, who has had a magnificent show career. This bitch shows the proud high head carriage so valued in the USA, with a level topline and strong, elegant sweep to the quarters

molars are all present. It is definitely a time-consuming task but I feel that this check is becoming more and more necessary in our breed, since, as it becomes increasingly 'civilised' in its feeding habits, so more teeth are failing to appear, in particular the pre-molars. It is, however, just one fault among many to be assessed and considered by the judge.

While your puppy is growing up to showing age take the opportunity of going to dog shows where Afghan classes are scheduled.

SHOWING

With luck there may even be a breed show in your area. Information about forthcoming shows can be found in the two dog journals *Dog World* and *Our Dogs* and the secretary of area breed clubs will be pleased to let you know where you can go to see Afghans being judged in the vicinity.

Study the whole ring procedure of how the dogs enter the ring and the exhibitors collect their ring cards from the steward. When the dogs have been arranged round the ring note how they, one by one, come before the judge, how they stand to allow a great deal of handling, and how each owner tries to present his dog to the best advantage to the judge. Imagine yourself in that ring and try to marshal the order of events: placing your dog; a quick smooth down; putting down the grooming brush which can be an added distraction and encumbrance; how to place the lead so that it doesn't spoil the line of your hound. Decide whether you could allow him to stand freely, whether you would need a fairly tight lead or would it just be necessary to hold him under the chin. In other words, think carefully about the whole process and practise it with your puppy so that when you enter the ring you are not a quivering mass of confusion. If there are any ring-training classes in your area these would be most helpful to both you and your dog. Breed secretaries will be pleased to assist with information.

Listen carefully to the exhibitors' talk around the ringside: many helpful hints can be picked up from their criticisms of other handlers in the ring, and also about preparation. If you hear derogatory remarks about the kennel from which you bought your dog, do not worry, an amazing amount of frustrations are disposed of by a bit of malicious criticism and you know your own dog is super. Also, strangely enough, outside the competition we are all quite remarkably friendly and helpful to each other.

When your puppy is about five months, start to look in the papers for shows for which he will be eligible at six months. Then write to the secretary for a schedule and enter him in the breed classes for minor puppy or puppy. If breeds are scheduled, you will have to enter him in the appropriate breed class. If Afghan puppy classes are not available you will still be able to enter the variety puppy class. Here you will meet puppies of all breeds, some far more speedily maturing than yours and, in fact, some may even be challenge certificate winners.

Some societies send out exhibitors' passes, other smaller ones do not. The championship-show secretaries invariably do. You can send a stamped addressed card for the secretary of the show to return to you and this proves they have received your entry.

The day before the show, bath your dog. Groom him out to perfection before you actually place him in the bath since you do not want to create a solid mat anywhere, then bath him with a very good quality shampoo. There are a great many really lovely dog-coat preparations for sale but a human one for soft fly-away hair is equally good.

When shampooing, smooth the hair downwards all the time. Do not rub in too many directions and thus cause tangling but make sure that every scrap of dirt or grease is removed at all layers. Give two shampoos and rinse out very thoroughly, being careful not to get soap and water into his eyes. Then use a conditioner. Rub it in and allow it to stand on the coat for the required number of minutes, comforting meanwhile, your wet clammy dog. Rinse out again and gently wring the water out of the coat, allowing it to lie as flat as possible. Soak up as much surplus water in towels as you can but do not frantically rub around in all directions. He has a lot of work and grooming ahead of him so try to avoid any unnecessary tangling. Puppy coats, though not so glamorous have their own consolations, they are not such awfully hard work as the adult coats.

Dry with a hair-dryer, gently brushing the coat sideways and downwards so that the hot air will dry the coat and allow it to fall straight. Do not try to cope with too large a section at once – think of a hairdresser doing a blow wave.

When all is dry, a suitable coat spray can be used, depending upon the coat's maturity. Adult coats often look best with a spray containing mink oil which gives a silky sheen and prevents the hair from flying.

A puppy coat should remain soft and fluffy and not be plastered down. Do not at this point lose sight of the fact that he is a hunting hound. Beautiful, yes. Effeminate, no.

SHOWING

Incidentally, to promote the best growth of ear fringes, it is always advisable to train your dog from puppyhood to wear a snood when eating. This prevents the ears from getting in the food dish, particularly as they grow longer, and your dog will not wake in the night and chew his ear fringes completely away while enjoying a midnight snack. Most gorgeous, glamorous elasticated snoods can be ordered from Mary Rogers of California, who supplies them around the world, or you can make your own with a close-fitting tube of stretch material which encloses the head, neck and ears from just behind the eyes to the base of the neck. The easiest to make, but not so effective for a very boisterous hound, is a length cut from a stocking.

By now you will know how good your dog is at travelling. If he is going to arrive upset and bothered from the journey, administer a light sedative, supplied by your vet, but only as much as is required to lessen his anxiety and stop him dribbling. (You will probably find the slight drying tendency will make him need a small drink on arrival at the show.) If you do have to give him any such help, do arrive at the show as early as possible so that any bad effects will have worn off and he will not be at all drowsy or wobbly in the ring. He will need every atom of intelligence and wit in today's hot competition.

If your showing necessitates long journeys and overnight stops, ascertain beforehand at which hotels you can take your Afghan in your room. Most hotels allow them in the bedrooms and, if they behave themselves, seem really glad to see such beautiful creatures. Motels also seem very reasonable about having them indoors and I have actually bathed one in a motel bathroom. For the sake of the reputation of the breed, however, be sensible and see that he is well exercised and that he has a large enough sleeping blanket to remove the possibility of dirty pawmarks on the furniture or the carpets. They are so noticeable that their peccadilloes seem more obvious than most.

Your dog bag, packed the night before, should include your grooming equipment of brushes – the wire brush and Maison Pearson bristle and nylon mixture – a comb and coat spray. A tin of talcum powder in case of muddy or dirty looking paws is invaluable and a large towel in case of rain or puddles. Do not forget to pack his water bowl and a bottle of water in case it is difficult to find a supply and remember his bag of titbits. If you are planning an overnight stay do not forget his snood and the tin-opener if you intend to feed canned food; this is where American exhibitors score over us with their preference for dried, easily packaged food. In my dog bag I also put my exhibitor's pass (if there is one) and my schedule so that I know exactly where I am going and cannot make any mistake about the time. Incidentally, it is often advisable to keep a perfume bottle handy in case the dog gets a whiff of a bitch in season.

For a benched show you will need a bench blanket for him to lie on. This should be about a metre square so that it can easily be folded to fit a large or small bench. Try to supply a colour or pattern which really shows off your dog to advantage. If it is not a benched show then bring a blanket big enough for him to sprawl out on without getting his coat dusty and dirty on the ground.

Once arrived at the show and having parked either in the official car park, or in a suitable place so that you do not return to find your car towed away, have your pass ready and purchase your catalogue on the way in. This contains the bench number of the exhibits and also states the number of the ring in which they will be judged.

Deal first with your dog. See that he is firmly chained onto his bench and settled down cosily on his blanket before starting to have a long chat with anyone. With luck you will have time for him to relax and have a breather before serious grooming out need commence. Put your bag neatly under the bench and do not leave handbags or valuables of any description lying around, nor your catalogue where the dog can chew it. Even brushes and catalogues are fair game to some fortune hunters if left lying on the bench. Once the dog is settled relax for a few minutes yourself, ascertain that there is no need for a panic hurry then give him a leisurely groom out and a small drink so that he only needs a smoothing down to go into the ring. At the same time pick up any fluff that has dropped and do not leave it lying around. We Afghan exhibitors have acquired a very bad name for mess.

Do not let your dog drink a lot just before he has to run around in the ring. It must be most uncomfortable for him to have a large quantity of water slopping around inside all the time he is showing off his paces.

Make sure that your ring clip or pin is at the ready to hold your ring number and all you have to do is wait for your class. Time passes very quickly and pleasantly when chatting to the other exhibitors and meeting their dogs.

Be ready in good time for your class, enter the ring at the opening provided and, if ring numbers have not been placed on the benches, tell the ring steward your number and he will give you your ring card which you display prominently on your person. There will at this point be a huge crowd all wanting the same thing but do not be impatient. The steward will tell everyone where to stand the dogs in line and usually the judge walks around and gives the class the once-over before commencing going over all the exhibits individually. At this stage you can allow your dog to relax, particularly if it is a puppy. Then, when there are only about two exhibits between you and the judges, start to prepare him. The responsibility for being ready to enter your class lies entirely with you, not the steward, although an efficient one will chase up laggard exhibitors. When it is your turn, stand your dog, carefully stacked, before the judge, who will then proceed to examine him and ask the puppy's age. Do have that pat. Do not have to count it off on your fingers!

The judge will ask you to move your dog in exactly the same manner in which the other dogs have been moved, either straight up and down, or in a triangle, or all round the ring. If you have watched the proceedings, it will all be very simple. Just listen carefully. After your dog has been seen you will return to the end of the line and about two dogs before the finish start to prepare your dog to stand while the judge makes a last tour of inspection before choosing his winners and making his awards.

If you are lucky enough to be called out into the centre of the ring stack your dog once more; the judge will probably not have made a final decision as yet, so 'showing' and showmanship are still necessary. If you win a second placing the first-prize winner's owner will be delighted should you think fit to congratulate him.

Prize cards and rosettes may be displayed above your bench but take care to remove any money or vouchers that may be attached to the card before you put it up.

Best-of-breed awards and special prizes such as best puppy can take many forms and colours. There are superb rosettes, sashes, pennants and even satin dog coats with jewelled trimmings. There is no hard-and-fast rule and dog societies have varied ideas. You would find it is far different in the States however. Even the best-of-breed awards are laid down as to size and appearance, even to the width of the ribbons, and the American Kennel Club representative present will check that there is no discrepancy. He will incidentally see that the judging procedure, conduct and running of the whole show comes up to required standards. There are also wonderful class awards which can be kept forever, unlike our perpetual trophies held only from show to show. American trophies take the form of magnificent statuettes, rose bowls, silver salvers – in fact a plethora of largess abounds. Our own Kennel Club does not send an official representative but relies on the officers and committee of each canine society to provide a smoothly run show and any discrepancies are reported to them by the secretary afterwards. There is an official procedure for complaints, dealt with at a later date by the Kennel Club, but the very dedicated dog folk of Great Britain spend an enormous amount of time and effort behind the scenes to provide such superbly smooth-running events.

The Continental shows are less flamboyant but most have delightful trophies, as do the Scandinavian countries. They also have their shows benched in a similar manner to ours. The US tends to go in for only a few benched shows proportionately, and keeps dogs crated in the areas provided, while the crates double as grooming tables. Here the show folk take their folding tables and chairs; sunshades and portable dog pens for an outside show and they are all able to socialise and have a really enjoyable time themselves. The dogs, however, are not so officially on display as in the UK on rigid rows of benching. Incidentally, bear in mind that your dog is only allowed off its bench for actual grooming, showing and exercise for up to a quarter of an hour. You may also only allow the specifically numbered dog on each bench, not pop its best friend on to keep it company.

It is quite permissible for you to ask the judge for an opinion of your dog after he has completed his judging and has picked out his final winner but you may not hold any conversation in the ring. Some judges still have the courage of their convictions and are willing to walk around the benches afterwards and talk to exhibitors. Nevertheless remember that, even if you did not win, there is no need for animosity; obviously the judge preferred someone else's dog, but if there was no competition and everyone thought alike there would be no purpose in holding dog shows.

Anyway there is always another day. Another show.

When you finally pack your bag, say goodbye, and depart, remember to leave no litter – and don't forget your dog!

8
Judging

Nowadays, when almost all canine societies, large and small, hold up to three shows a year, and almost always put on Afghan classes, it seems remarkably easy for anyone who knows a committee member or 'knows someone who knows someone else' to gain a judging appointment. Judges frequently appear in the ring relatively unknown to many exhibitors who have been showing Afghans for only a year or two. It is felt by many serious-minded people with the welfare of the breed at heart that these newcomers, although full of enthusiasm and a burning determination to see fair play and to right the wrongs of a dog consistently not placed, cannot in so short a time fully realise the physical implications behind the breed standard. Can they fully understand the underlying factors that cause a dog to move in a particular way, what gives it those unique breed characteristics, what structure lies beneath the flowing coat and why? In fact, have they the experienced judgement to weigh the assets and faults of one dog against another?

It is an undoubted fact that the whole atmosphere and structure of the society that frequents dog shows must give rise to this premature conviction of adequate knowledge. All those who care to listen have ample opportunity to hear constant streams of ringside commentaries by so many. There are the most comprehensive criticisms of dogs and judges, easy talk of hocks and stifles, pasterns and fallaways, shoulder placement and rear angulation, that it soon becomes an easy patter one can copy with spurious assurance.

It is interesting to note however that so often the criticism in such circles is rarely kindly but frequently denigrates hounds, handlers and judges. It is obviously considered most clever and

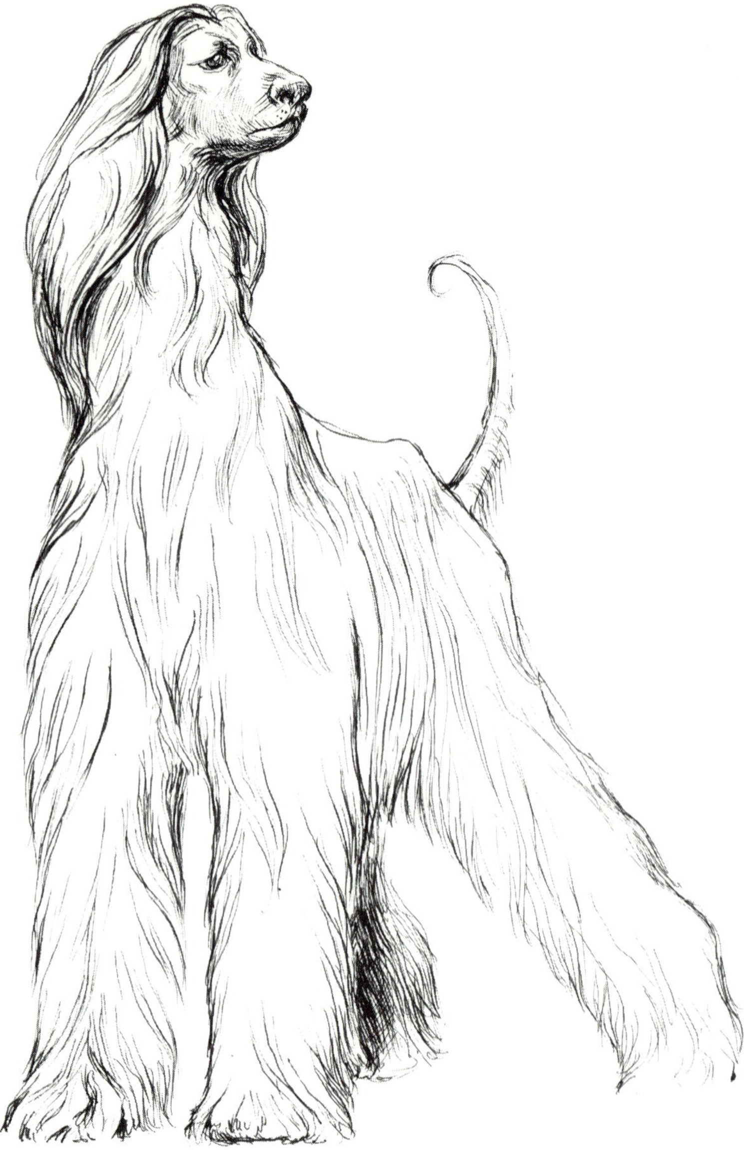

knowledgeable to find more faults than anyone else; virtues are found to be, if not entirely non-existent, then at least negligible.

It is a sad fact that a little knowledge is truly a dangerous thing and such people do not realise they have barely begun to learn.

Knowledge is of tantamount importance to any judge, however small the show, and however new a recruit he may be to the ranks of judges.

It is essential to know the standard fully and this can only be managed by constantly rereading it and considering its implications with regard to one's own dog and others (but beware of making some brash statement with regard to the conformation of someone's pride and joy). It can be further increased by reading, in conjunction with the standard, some of the excellent books available on conformation and the standard and movement and by constant discussion with really knowledgeable judges and breeders.

Tom Horner states in his book *Take them round, please*:

> Knowledge, deciveness, integrity and the rest of the necessary qualities are useless without one vital possession — an 'eye for a dog', which is the ability that every good judge has to recognise at a glance whether a dog is right or wrong, good, bad or indifferent. A priceless gift, without which no one can make a real success of judging, it is acquired by long and painstaking study of anatomy, Breed Standards, high-class dogs and poor ones, breed books, photographs and so on, until it becomes an instinctive skill to weigh up the merits of a dog almost on first sight. The history of the breeds, their development over the years, discussions with breeders and judges, all help to give the student this vital eye for a dog.

Recently I was driving a fellow judge in the West Country where we were going to officiate as examiners at a test for aspiring judges. During our journey he produced a copy of the breed standard and we went through it in great detail, each coming up with aspects that we had not previously considered consciously in precisely that fashion. Both learnt something fresh.

On this occasion one candidate taking the test for the second time was obviously somewhat at sea and gave distinctly hazy answers to our questions about the breed and its construction. Afterwards this person asked for guidance in passing the examination in the future and I suggested that it might be an advantage to learn the standard more thoroughly. To this they replied that it was unnecessary as they already knew it, having learnt it for their first attempt at the exam. I therefore mentioned the manner in which my co-judge and I had passed a large portion of our journey, to be met with a disbelieving stare which turned into a knowing look which said as plainly as if shouted out loud, 'They didn't know the standard sufficiently well, they needed to swot it up to come here at all.'

It was said of the late Fred Cross, one of the great judges of our time, and also one of the most courteous and kindly of the all-rounders, that every night when he went to bed he read through one of the breed standards – if only some of our aspiring newest judges could approach the matter with such humility!

On a par with knowledge I am also of the opinion that courage is one of the true essentials of a judge's make-up.

A newcomer at his first engagement is probably only too well aware that standing at the ringside are all his acquaintances waiting to see him meet out justice to their dogs and others and make sure that dogs frequently 'put down' receive the wins that they are sure they deserve. How often may he have concurred that Mrs So-and-So was winning only on her reputation and not on the quality of her dog. When the great day comes therefore and he goes over the dogs, will he have the courage to give it to the best whether it really turns out to be the famous winner or a little known dog with an unknown owner?

There is also the fact that sooner or later one's friends are going to appear in the ring. The answer to this is simple, if your friend's dog is the best, then it must 'go up'. If it is not of the same quality as the others then it should, regardless of friendship, go down. Friendship must never embarrass you. As Horner puts it:

> The mental quality most needed is that of calm detachment: a judge must be able to make up his mind about the dogs before him despite all the pressures that will from time to time confront him. He must not allow himself to be swayed by any other considerations. It is just as dis-

honest to put down his best friend's dog in order to demonstrate how impartial he is, as it is to put up for friendship's sake. And the same goes for judging the dog of his worst enemy. It would be wrong to put it up just to show his impartiality. He is there to judge the dogs and for no other purpose.

Similarly, a judge may find himself in a quandary when confronted with animals he has bred himself. I know it is all too easy to fall over backwards to be scrupulously fair and to try not to be biased towards one's own breeding, but these dogs have the right to be judged without a built-in penalty. If they are the best in the ring they must be placed accordingly. If they are not, then have the courage to admit it by your lower placing, or even by not placing them at all.

Every judge should have sufficient conviction of his placings to be able to disregard the frowns, glares, sneers and mutters that emanate from some disgruntled exhibitors. You will find that some are remarkably lacking in sportsmanship and good manners and some will try all sorts of tricks to get a first placing, running in front of the exhibit the judge was pulling out, stepping on, or in front of handler and dog. Sometimes it needs a lot of courage to put these determined people back in their place but it must be done, regardless of any repercussions and one should always remember that the Kennel Club will support judges against threats, blows and slanderous statements. The judge must be master of his ring.

I quote Stafford Sommerfield's writing in *Dog World*:

> What surprises me more than ill mannered exhibitors, is that a judge is prepared to put up with it. There is only one thing to do. Write down the exhibitor's number and make a report to the show secretary, giving the name of a witness.
>
> It is intolerable that judges should be treated like this, while doing a job as best they are able. One understands the disappointment of exhibitors who think they know better (they may or may not do so) but they have to be taught good manners and sportsmanship.

At the end of judging it will be very obvious who is feeling upset and who isn't. Those that you have considered as friends may be conspicuous by their absence, some will turn away at your approach, others will have a few terse, bitter words to utter. The fact must be faced that, however careful and scrupulous you are in your judging, people will undoubtedly find fault somewhere; you cannot please everyone and some 'friends' will undoubtedly be lost. If the thought upsets you, then refuse the engagement in the first place.

In some respects it may be a disadvantage to judge, since in these days of enormous entries it must be remembered that at most open shows, one dog in each class actually wins while three or four others are placed. At championship shows one wins again while five or six are placed, depending upon the generosity in cards and rosettes of the show committee. In our breed it is not at all rare for there to be classes of fifty to sixty dogs and then a large proportion of people are liable to be upset to varying degrees, and at the end, when you have weeded out your winners to your best of breed, you may be made quite painfully aware that you have one friend only, who at that moment will be sporting the best-of-breed rosette.

It is quite possible that you may have irate owners dashing after you as you leave the ring, wanting to know why you did not put up their most beautiful hound. You may, after judging 300 dogs (or more) have people from lower classes of up to sixty exhibits pestering you to remember all you could about their beloved pet who did not gain a placing but was one of the many black-masked goldens, looking much alike in the crush along the ringside. All these must be met with courtesy, consideration and (even after six or seven hours in the ring on your feet and a steadily increasing sinking tiredness) an unfailing good temper, regardless of innuendoes about your intelligence and eyesight.

During judging it is not unknown to hear voices raised in tones of pained astonishment discussing the quality of your line-ups, and surprise at your general lack of ability. If you are really engrossed they rarely impinge upon your consciousness, but they can prove hurtful to a sensitive novice.

Please realise judging is not all kudos and publicity but occasionally an endurance test.

Ch Bondor Serenade, owned and bred by Allan Brooks and Eric Swallow, shown winning her third Championship at the age of twenty-three months. A bitch of extraordinarily sound conformation and flowing movement, she was sired by Ch Wazir of Desertaire. The author is proud that she started Serenade off as a winner at her first show and gave her Best of Breed at her last appearance in the ring

Speaking as a judge I am convinced that we all at some time in our career go through a stage of feeling that we know far more than is actually so, and only gradually with a great deal of experience do we realise how scant our knowledge really is. It is at that point that we start learning in earnest.

I remember so clearly my first judging appointment in Alexandra Palace and the thrill and utter enjoyment of handling all the exhibits (a feeling that I still experience at all the shows I judge)

and I also remember later when my excitement had died down and I sat down to write my report that I realised I did not know as much as I had liked to think and that in particular I was not sure enough about what makes a really good front.

It was at that show that a lovely young bitch made her debut in puppy and I had the honour of awarding her her first red card. She went on to become that famous champion, Bonder Serenade, and I also had the pleasure of putting her best of breed at her very last appearance at Bath Championship Show in 1968.

My best of breed at this first show that I judged was a super young dog who later became English and Australian Ch Waliwog of Carloway. I had completely fallen for him when I first met him as a four-month old carrying his teddy bear around in Sheila Devitt's garden at the Carloway kennels so maybe I was a little prejudiced, but I shall never forget how exercised I was in my mind between the choice of 'Wiggy' — as he was affectionately known — and a splendid stubborn young fellow of most sound construction who went on to become Ch Jali of Vishnu, who on that day, as on so many other occasions, dug his toes in and was a devil to move in the ring.

The most important effect of my first show, after that taste of being in the hot spot after five years of showing and earlier years of just owning was that it gave added impetus to my determination to do everything in my power to learn all that I could in order to become worthy of the title of judge. I am still learning.

All who wish to judge should ask themselves, 'Why do I want to judge?'

Do you feel that this is an essential stage in one's progress towards making up a champion? Are you really doing it for your own sake and not thinking of what you may be able to give to the breed? There is a popular misconception that judging invariably consists of a two-way exchange — that you put up someone's dog and in return they will put up yours. This can happen but on the whole I like to think that it does not. As one who has, over the years, done a fair amount of judging at all levels, I am convinced that I have not received any favours, although I may have remained blissfully unaware of it. However, we still remember with hilarity

JUDGING

the proof of the non-existence of the reciprocal system through the year that I could not go to Crufts, since, although I judged at two championship shows during the qualifying year beforehand not one of the judges, all who intended to show under me, liked my dog well enough to ignore his stubborn behaviour in the ring and give him the necessary first prize. Quite frankly I do not think it possible for anyone to put up a convincing show in the ring with one eye on the handler and the other on the exhibit.

Do you feel you have sufficient experience and understanding of the breed to select and put up really good dogs, the best in the class, regardless of the reputation of those standing in the ring before you? Remember that people will always try to win with a slightly inferior hound, trusting to the fact that you may not be able to recognise it inside that flowing coat. It really comes down at times to a battle of wits between the judge and a skilful handler.

Are you prepared to shoulder the responsibility of knowing that what you do today in the ring may in time to come actually affect the future of our breed? Do you appreciate that your choice of winners is in the public eye and that from such dogs are chosen the next generation of stud dogs and brood bitches, that you could well actively contribute to the making or marring of a stud dog's career or the subsequent breeding of a whole line?

If, after such considerations, you feel you can offer something to the breed as well as taking from it yourself then go ahead, judge, do your best, but always hold a post mortem and be determined to do even better next time.

More and more breed societies are endeavouring to give instruction to aspiring judges. In my own club, after four years of active participation in the breed, candidates can attend lectures on varying aspects of the Afghan giving a basic knowledge of what is involved in the standard and how it applies to construction and movement. They are also instructed on the order and control of their ring and the duties of a steward. Then comes guidance in handling and actual judging by championship-status judges, who willingly give their time to train them and hand on their knowledge, painstakingly acquired in a hard school over many years. Sadly only a minority appreciate the amount of time and effort given by these few genuinely dedicated people with the interests of the breed at heart. These same judges not only lecture but travel hundreds of miles to examine candidates and spend hours afterwards marking papers. All the time they have a single thought in mind – not remuneration since they are lucky to even cover their expenses – 'the good of the breed'.

Having passed the exam, the junior judge may have his name placed on the junior list and be eligible to judge limited and open shows, not only for general canine societies but also for the balloted club shows.

In England we do not have student judges in the ring while classes are in progress. However, this does occur on the Continent and while I was judging in Barcelona a young man was put under my care who watched every move I made while going over the dogs and asked searching questions about all the points I was looking out for under their coats. In our numerically large breed I doubt that we would have the time and opportunity to help such candidates at our championship shows but it would certainly be an idea to adopt at smaller shows. Meanwhile our students are encouraged to steward, for in the ring they can acquire knowledge from the judge they are helping and also learn ring management from first-hand experience.

After six active years in the breed and after having judged six open shows or thirty-six Afghan classes – as well as having exhibited a dog to entry in the stud book – a judge may progress to the open list, from which members ballot for judges for club open shows. Judging of any Afghan club's open show or a general canine society's show with ten consecutive classes gives the entrée to the championship-show list once the candidate has had ten years in the breed and got three of his dogs into the stud book.

Once on a club's championship list it is possible to be voted to judge at that club's annual championship show, the most signal honour since it is the members' choice, not just the committee's. They may also be considered by the Kennel Club for any championship show to which they have been nominated. The only other hurdle to be overcome is acceptance by the Kennel Club of information given on their questionnaire.

Having finally made the grade, they are entitled to award that coveted green and white certificate which states 'I am clearly of the opinion that (name) is of such outstanding merit as to be worthy of the title of Champion' and to which, for better or for worse, they append their name. One hopes that all future judges realise this is an action not to be lightly undertaken for any dog winning a challenge certificate (known as a ticket) is a potential popular stud dog, and every bitch winning the same certificate will undoubtedly be marked down as the producer of future winning progeny.

In actual fact each judge finds in bold lettering at the beginning of his judging book an admonition from the Kennel Club to the effect that the certificate must be withheld if no dog is of sufficient merit for the award. Rarely has the occasion arisen when the challenge certificate has been withheld and I have then heard points for and against the judge's action, but to the disappointed exhibitors it has not been a popular one.

Exhibitors have the right to expect extremely high standards of judges of their breed. Not only have they paid a fee of considerable proportions to have their dog 'gone over' by the judge, they have also paid him a compliment by allowing him to handle and criticise their much valued Afghan. Therefore the judge must see that every dog receives adequate attention even though it is often obvious that some exhibits could never merit a placing.

The judge should also have a care to waiting dogs, and in many of our large classes, with entries queuing up possibly for more than an hour to be seen, they should not have to stand on edge for the whole time. Our Kennel Club has a rule against splitting large classes but there is no reason at all why half cannot be sent to one side of the ring to relax while half are examined, the halves then changing over, provided that no dogs are pulled out or comparisons made before all dogs are present and seen.

In the States there is a better arrangement. Once the class has entered the ring and has, as it were, come under judges' orders, he may instruct the steward to escort half the exhibits and their handlers to a special enclosed area, usually in a quiet and shady place where they remain relaxed and comfortable in the steward's care, then the other half is sent out and finally they all return to the ring

International Ch Tzara of Pooghan, owned and bred by Mr Dennis McCarthy. A most beautiful and stylish bitch of unsurpassed showmanship, she was for sometime the record holder in the breed and won twenty-one Challenge Certificates, thus beating Rifka's Musquat D'Rar. She also won five green stars in Ireland for the selection of the winners. No judge should harshly penalise a dog for relaxing for a while. The onus is on the exhibitor, however, to place the dog smoothly back into position at a second's notice when they see the judge looking around for comparisons or to refresh his memory. I well recall when going over a specials' class in Texas how enthralled I was by a tall, elegant, well made black and tan with great personality and ring presence, presented to such perfection that whenever I came near to finding a fault that I suspected might be there I found that dog just pulled up, moved slightly so that I could not be sure. After seeing several more dogs I decided to take another look at that dog while it relaxed. I turned smartly and, my goodness, so did that handler. In the flicker of a whisker the dog was poised and perfect but I had managed to see what I wanted.

One of the most frequent grouses about judges is that they are, in moments of indecision, too prone to move exhibits too many times round the ring. Let us face facts honestly, a well made hound can cope easily, no matter how many times he is moved; the well made exhibitor is liable to have a heart attack if sent on the same marathon as the hound. There should not be any need for fifth or even sixth thoughts.

Equally, when on the move, it is galling for any exhibitor to glance at the judge to make sure that they are not running in the wrong direction, in a ring that feels a mile long, only to find that he is having a quiet chat with his steward or, worse, with a ringsider, and hasn't looked in their direction at all.

I have always felt it most important that any judge should be obviously confident, in complete command and definitely enjoying his task. Worry and fear cannot exist if he has made sure that he possesses all relevant knowledge and no one lacking in self-confidence should ever allow themselves to be manoeuvered into the centre of the ring. The engagement has been entered voluntarily and exhibitors do not expect a morose glare or sullen attitude.

Courtesy to the exhibitors is of paramount importance and it does not take a second to smile and say thank you to an exhibitor when you send a dog back to its place after examination. It has always been my contention (though not of many others) that when a judge has finally picked his winners he should not summarily hand over the others to his steward without a glance, and a muttered 'I've done with these' or even 'Get rid of that lot.' A smile round the ring and a thank you shows that you appreciated them, even if you could not place their dogs.

Show secretaries also expect points from judges. When you are asked to judge, reply promptly in writing in order to avoid confusion. If you expect a fee or expenses notify them at the same time since small societies might not be able to afford you. If, through some unforeseen circumstances, you really cannot judge after all give as much notice as possible. There may be circumstances under which the Kennel Club could query the fact that a judge did not fulfil an engagement, under rule 25, section A.

There is, of course, another side to the coin, namely, what has the judge the right to expect from exhibitors?

No judge should be expected to go over a dog which is liable to take his hand off if he tries to handle its head, or indeed any other part of its anatomy. No exhibitor should ever be so unfair or foolhardy as to bring a dog of uncertain temperament into the ring. It should also be remembered that there is a Kennel Club rule that no conversation is allowed with the judge, and that no one wants to hear, suddenly hissed into their ear 'this one's father is so-and-so's champion' or 'he was best in show last week under your best friend'. It tends to make one feel very antagonistic!

Similarly the dogs to be handled should have been bathed or, failing that, thoroughly groomed and cleaned. Once, to my horror, an exhibitor spat upon his hands very thoroughly and proceeded to dampen down a flyaway coat. Fortunately there was soap and water – but how frequently show secretaries neglect to supply a towel.

Exhibitors would do well to remember that they have paid voluntarily for the judge's opinion of their dog. Having received that opinion by virtue of the placing of the dogs there is no need to glower, snarl or make rude and audible remarks or tear up your card. You have received exactly what you paid for – an opinion. If you do not like it then you have no need to enter under the particular judge again.

There are also pin pricks when little time is available for each dog. Do be prompt into the ring; make sure that you are wearing your correct ring number and make sure that it is easily seen.

Finally, while on the subject of rights and expectations, what should the *dog* expect? He is really the most important part of the show yet so often the one least considered.

He expects firm but gentle handling from the judge. He does not want his ears turned inside out, fingers in his eyes, his mouth rudely yanked open and his head nearly torn from his body. Nor does he expect his tail to be dislocated, his feet pulled from under him or his testicles squeezed to pulp. He is a feeling, living, intelligent creature and must be treated with care and consideration. He needs to be allowed to relax during judging of other dogs, be told clearly and firmly what to do – not hit, shouted at or scolded – and under no circumstances when he leaves the ring beaten because he has lost. So many of us have seen the sly kick, the slaps with the hair brush from a disappointed exhibitor and I have several times had to warn people in the ring to have a care. There is, of course, the plain naughty dog who suddenly decides to misbehave in the ring and has the handler's nerves in shreds. He obviously needs a sterner tone when he refuses to stand but it should never be repeated when he leaves the ring. It means nothing then.

Lastly he expects a kind word and a cuddle when he has finished working for his owner, whether he has won or lost. He is mentally on a par with a child and his greatest delight is to do something that pleases you.

When the day of your first judging appointment finally dawns make sure that you allow yourself plenty of time to get to the show. Go straight to the secretary's office or table and find out where you will be judging. You are usually allowed to provide your own steward; in that case inform the secretary when you accept the appointment. Your envelope or box with the prize cards, ring cards, rosettes and judging book will be given to you with a catalogue – for the steward's use, not yours. Although the Kennel Club has no definite rule against it, a look at the catalogue beforehand would be a most unpopular move.

You may, of course, look at your judging book to see the size of your classes and, if in doubt about how to fill it in, ask your steward or someone familiar with such things. It is a simple little booklet with the ring numbers written in three columns. One is for your own use and the other two are made to be torn out for the secretary's records and the award board. All you have to do is mark the winner's placings by their numbers.

The steward will organise your ring under your instructions. Therefore make it clear to him in which corner you want the dogs seen in previous classes, in which direction you want the dogs to move and anything else that you consider to be relevant. Although in the long run the onus is entirely on your shoulders, a good steward is of tremendous assistance. Instruct him to make sure that dogs already seen and entered from another class are assembled in winning order. You may also ask him whether two winners in different classes have already met in any class or whether they have met any of the other unbeaten dogs — but try to check this yourself if you are in any doubt. A bad decision is your responsibility. Always be on the alert to make sure that you do not accidentally place a dog in front of one that has already been placed above it in a previous class. If of course a good dog which had to be unplaced, because it dug its toes in, later moved magnificently in another class, then you would be entitled to place it above others this second time around.

Most judges begin by walking round quietly taking stock of the Afghans before them. This can commence as the dogs enter the ring and a great deal can be seen while the last exhibits are being collected. At this point also it is usual to check with the steward to ascertain that all dogs already seen in a previous class are duly placed in order in their corner.

Judging procedure is very personal in all aspects. You may always move the exhibits round a couple of times in a large circle or just concentrate on movement during assessment. Each dog in turn comes forward and when placed in position it is advisable to step back and assess the balance of the animal by looking at it from all angles so that the whole of it can be clearly seen. Then make an evaluation of the dog with respect to the standard by examining its head for balance and a prominent occiput, shape and set of eyes, ear placement, amount of stop in the foreface, Roman nose and correctness of bite and underjaw. Gently stretch the neck to see the length, examine the shoulder for width and layback, check the musculature of the back and body and see whether the topline is dippy or otherwise. Next consider the shape of the ribs together with depth, the actual ending of the rib cage and the length, width and muscle formation of the loin. There should also be a check to see if there is adequate width to the chest between the forelegs, and a judge who knows his business will run his hands down the foreleg from the shoulder to check the angulation and length of the upper arm, the proportion of the forearm, slope and spring of pastern, and lift the paw to find its size, and the arch of the toe. The hindquarters will be considered from the hips to ascertain their prominence, the width between them, the angle and length of the fall-away or croup, as well as the length of the upper and lower thigh, the angulation at the stifle and the strength of the muscles with a quick check to make sure that the dog is entire (that is, with both testicles descended into the scrotum). Finally the length and proportion of the leg from the hock to the rear of the foot will be measured with probably a gentle push at the os calcis to test for slipping hocks and a quick check to see that the pads are firmly placed on the ground. This latter is a good guide to correct foot shape and stance. This all sounds a very lengthy and complicated business but it is comparatively speedy to one who knows his job. Every judge needs a pattern and everyone has a slightly different theory. Some start at the head, go down the neck directly to the forequarters. Alternatively one can deal with the front first, then the body, then the rear end. Or one can make a complete square of the outline by taking the head, neck, topline, hindquarters, back along the body to the forequarters and ending with the front feet. If the whole handling process is completely automatic, so that one is not desperately trying not to forget to consider tail, loin or brisket then it leaves more concentration for committing the knowledge gained to memory for the moment when all dogs are judged and ready for placing.

After handling, each dog is moved round the ring according to the time and space available. If the entry is large and one is limited to a minute or so per dog then a triangle is the best solution and all the angles of movement are shown speedily to their best advantage (see illustration). With plenty of time it is pleasant to send the dog up and down twice in order to see it coming and going and then to see the thrust of the legs from the side (see illustration). If you really want to see a dog's movement on the turn then a T with several corners is the neatest solution (see illustration).

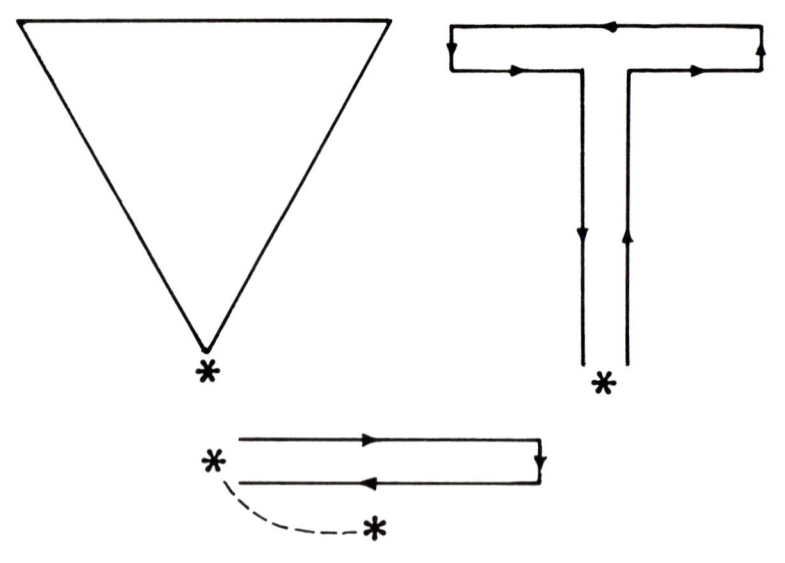

The triangle course and the T shape for the dog's movement means that the judge need move only fractionally to assess movement from all angles. The up and down is excellent when a dog can be moved twice and the judge has time to change position

In a large entry it is both permissible and desirable to make a quick note about movement since a fault in that department can easily be forgotten and in the case of an otherwise impressive dog can be overlooked in the last line-up. For example 'throws r.l.' which in my notes means throws rear left leg out, or 'H.K.' which means hocks knock. A couple of lines can remind me that the width at the breast bone is insufficient, elbows go in and the front feet splay outward during movement. Also, when faced with a lot of dogs, it helps to make a note of the exhibit's number and write 'yes' or 'no' on your judging book or note pad so that the ones you wish to see again can be called out with a minimum of fuss and wasted time.

Most judges pull out the best ten or so in a large class of thirty or more from which to make their final choice and pick their winners from these. Usually the first and the next two or three stand out very clearly from the rest. Sometimes it is desirable to move the exhibits again, either collectively or singly, and sometimes against another dog.

The Kennel Club lays down that exhibits must be placed in the centre of the ring in order of merit and also that placings must be awarded from left to right. They are usually turned to face the side of the ring where the majority of exhibitors can see them and their ring numbers clearly or where the judge can see them best without the sun shining in his eyes. Incidentally exhibits must be placed in the ring even if the judge withholds the prize cards.

The awards are then made. In England the colours are red for first, blue for second, yellow for third and green for reserve, with varying shades for very highly commended and highly commended. In the United States the first-prize colour is blue and the second is red and there are firmly regulated rules about colours for best in show awards, whereas here they can be all colours of the rainbow and range from rosettes of varying magnificence to gold encrusted sashes and jewelled and embroidered dog coats. On the Continent there are beautiful official prize cards following a definite pattern, which name the actual awards – good, very good and excellent.

In England judges have to place dogs only to the number of prize cards offered. These must cover placings from first to reserve but can vary from five placings to seven, according to the generosity of the society. On the Continent, however, it is obligatory to place the dogs from first to last.

When judging in the United Kingdom it is customary to make notes on the first two placings at an open show, and three at a championship show and then to write a report which is published in the dog press. Although there is no compulsion to do so, it is considered shabby conduct if no report is forthcoming and exhibitors are upset if they cannot read the judge's opinion of their exhibit, or alternatively, what led him to place someone else's dog higher than theirs. Take a tape recorder with you to record as many facts as you need quickly. Officially no critique is called for in the United States.

Scandinavia and the Continent require criticisms to be made on the spot on each dog, and when judging overseas it is vital to have a good interpreter who can understand and successfully translate doggy terms. In some places the criticism is actually handed to the owner in the ring, in others it is officially recorded and given later. Also, in Scandinavia there is an extra award called the honours prize, which can be given to any dog the judge feels worthy of being a champion. There can be several of these in one class.

In nearly every country on the Continent there is a slightly different requirement for champion status. In France, for example, it is necessary to win one of the three CACs in Paris. You could win innumerable ones in other places but without that one your dog could never get its title. Similarly in Spain one of the certificates must be won in Madrid.

CAC is a shortened version of the Certificate for Aptitude for Champion and is applicable to the country in which it is won. There is also an award open to champions, the CACIB Certificate of Aptitude to International Champion of Beauty.

The Afghan that wins open dog or bitch in these countries, all of which come under the jurisdiction of the FCI (Federation Cynologique Internationale), receives the CAC, the equivalent of the UK Challenge Certificate. He or she is then able to compete in the champions' class with those who are already titled. The winner of this class is then awarded the CACIB, after which the two compete for best of sex. The CACIB is not awarded at all shows however.

Facing page
USA Ch Khayam's Apollo, originally owned by Dr Doyle Rogers and now the property of Mr and Mrs Tully, is handled by a professional handler Eugene Blake. Apollo has had a most outstanding show career and became one of America's top dogs. He made a most superb picture in the ring with his free movement, proud carriage and beautifully groomed coat

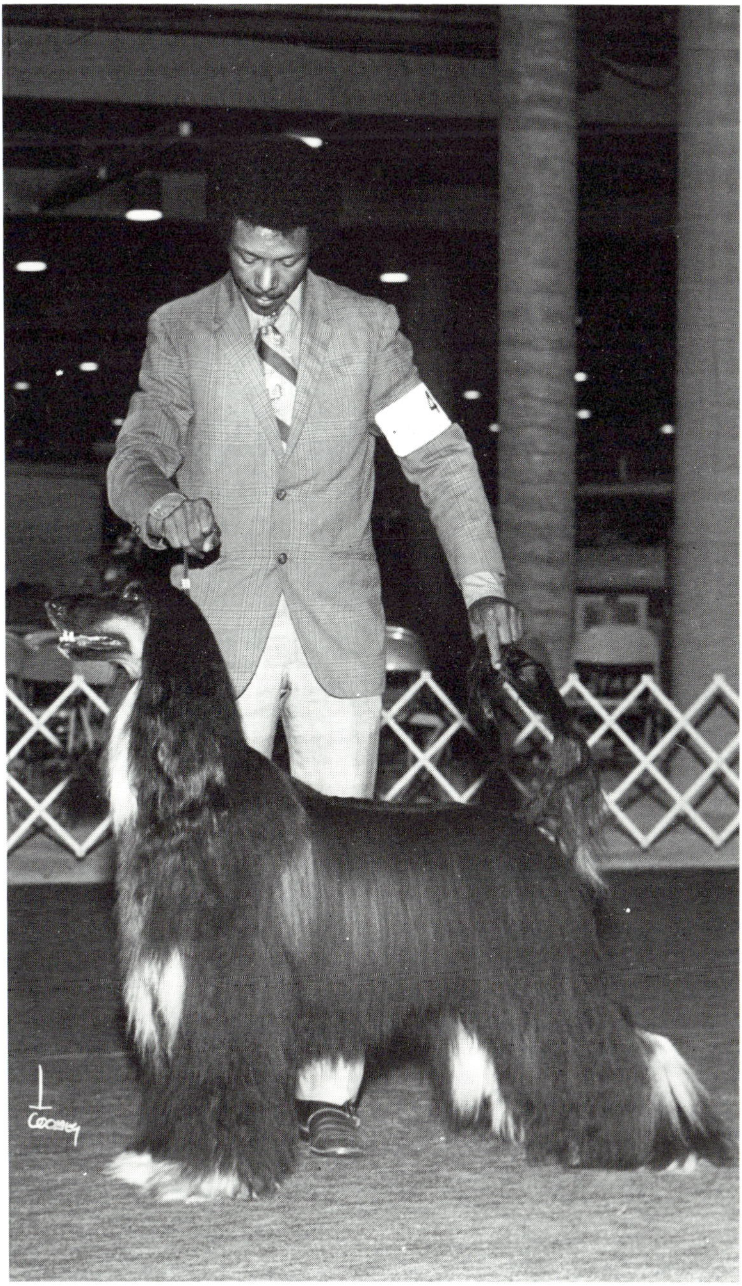

In America there is a similar method. All unbeaten dogs or bitches compete with each other to become winner's dog or winner's bitch. This one is able to compete in the specials or champions class for BOB. There is also a points' system, dependent on the number of dogs present and an Afghan can gain so many points to its title by becoming best winner of its sex at one of these shows, where the points awarded may be from three to five and an Afghan may become a champion of record upon the gaining of fifteen points.

In the UK all unbeaten dogs and bitches are asked for and since our exhibits are able to compete in more than one class it is quite possible to have fewer competing than one expects. The final choice then becomes best of sex and winner of the challenge certificate. Since we do not have a champions' class of any sort, our titled dogs are able to compete in the open class together with up-and-coming hopefuls. It is therefore much harder to become a champion in England, since competition is not spaced out in any way.

One more difference between the American style of judging and the British is that the judge generally makes a point, in the States, of picking out winners on the move, whereas on the whole in Britain, they stand in row for consideration. The American style is certainly a most stirring sight to see.

I cannot close this chapter without a request to all judges, male or female, not to let the side down in matters of sartorial splendour. Our Afghan rings attract enormous crowds and our judges are, on these occasions, the representatives of the human side of our breed. Moreover, exhibitors have spent hours grooming their dogs, judges should reciprocate. A slipshod appearance does not foster the idea of a crisp and workmanlike attitude, or indeed inspire confidence.

Big floppy hats that terrify dogs are out, so are furry cuffs that tempt every hound to mistake them for a rabbit, clanking chains, revealing necklines, and skirts that are far too short when you bend down. Likewise men should keep their hairy chests to themselves on a hot day and leave that sort of thing to the Afghans – they have a much more impressive growth anyway! Do remember that for long hours of standing and walking around the ring your shoes will need to be very comfortable indeed. Then, knowing that you are visually perfect, that you know your standard inside out and upside down, you can go into the ring with unfaltering confidence and nothing on your mind except the dogs in front of you.

Do your best, be completely honest and unbiased, disregard the other end of the lead and enjoy every minute of one of the most fascinating aspects of dogdom.

9
Origin and Development

There are many wild theories about the age of our breed and its origins. Many proudly boast this is the original dog that Noah took into the ark (the Saluki folk say the same thing, and we shall never know).

It has also been stated that Mohammed owned an Afghan (or Tazi) and therefore Afghans, unlike other mere dogs, are allowed into paradise. I once read a charming account of Mohammed's dog, with a long thick coat, decked with jewels who, before departing, took steps to ensure that his progeny remained on earth.

Whatever its origin it spreads with variations not only over Afghanistan itself but also through the surrounding districts.

There is a scarcity of old records although Major Mackenzie, a British officer, about 1888 stated that he had seen immense rock carvings depicting Afghan-like dogs in caves in Balkh with later inscriptions on them which could be dated back to Alexander the Great. No trace of these, or indeed of the caves, has since been rediscovered. As this is one of the most famous accounts with any historical reference to the breed it makes claims to the breed's antiquity very slender. Equally no one can prove that they are not as old as our wishful thinking would have them be.

One of the first pictures to show the breed, drawn in 1813 and since published so many times, was the delightful one of the 'Meenah of Jajurh with his Afghan Hound'. I always loved this as it so closely resembled one of my own little bitches, so feminine with an underlying mischief.

As the British army extended its activities over the frontier, so more was heard of the unique hounds mentioned by many names –

Afghan greyhound, Baluch hounds and Baruchzy (after the ruling family) hounds. They were also, in type, coupled with the Saluki and references were made to Persian greyhounds.

One of the most famous accounts comes from *Hutchinson's Dog Encyclopaedia* and tells of Afghans in Chaman:

> Chaman, you must know, is one of our principal posts on the North-West Frontier. A former Commander-in-Chief decreed that a post should be established at Chaman to be fed by a light railway from Quetta. Two mud forts guard the railway station, one on each side; each fort is manned by one company of Indian infantry, and one squadron native mounted levies and by dogs.
>
> What strikes the newcomer entering either of the forts at any hour

of the day is the large, extraordinary-looking creatures sprawling all over the place, fast asleep. In size and shape they somewhat resemble a large Greyhound, but such slight resemblance is dispelled by the tufts with which all are adorned: some having tufted ears, others tufted feet, and others, again, possessing tufted tails.

They are known as Baluchi Hounds, and they get their daily food ration from the commissariat babu; he is the only permanent resident of the fort. They will have no truck with any stranger, white or black.

When 'Retreat' sounds, the pack awakes, yawns, pulls itself together, and solemnly marches out to take up positions close to the newly arrived night guard. They appear to be under no leadership, yet as the patrols are told off a couple of dogs attach themselves to each patrol, and they remain with their respective patrols till 'reveille' next morning. Between a deep ditch and wall of the fort is a narrow path. Throughout the night, this path is patrolled by successive couples of dogs. Immediately one couple has completed the circuit of the walls and arrived back at the main gate, another couple starts out.

When it is remembered that these extraordinary hounds have never had any training whatsoever, that their duties are absolutely self-imposed – for no human being has the slightest control over them – the perfection of their organization and the smoothness with which they carry out their tasks make mere man gasp.

There is, I feel, no doubt at all that the Afghan came from a similar type of dog to the Saluki or the greyhound. Possibly they all had a common ancestor but it seems feasible that the dogs in this climatic area grew suitable coats to protect them from the fierce sun encountered during the day and the extreme cold at night. Indeed our own hounds, though now bred in what may seem ideal conditions, are still largely impervious to bitter weather, and can cope with some most unusually hot weather such as experienced in Britain in recent years.

The stronger type of jaw and head would also develop naturally – as well as through selective breeding – as a result of the way of life of generations of dogs bred and trained to hunt and kill.

There is no doubt that they were bred as hunters and there are many accounts of this. A letter of Mrs Amps, one of the first dedicated Afghan breeders, published in a Southern Afghan Club magazine states that:

Chipak, a red bitch, owned by Mrs Carter came from Princess Homaira in Afghanistan. The head is stronger and the eyes a little more full than is usually bred in the UK. She has a smooth coat and light feathering. The beautiful expression and the keen outlook are particularly noticeable

The Afghan Hound in his own country works for his living and that of his masters, and the same rule applies to the bitch. They are both trained to hunt deer and wolves, and also to course hares and foxes; in fact anything that will bring grist to their owner's mill. Incidentally, as night fell the latest recruit to our household became uneasy and anxious to go beyond the boundary of the Legation walls in order to hunt. We came to the conclusion that in many cases they were let loose to hunt for themselves at night-time. However, after a few days' good feeding they usually settled down quietly after the evening meal.

Mrs Joan Carter, wife of Mr Peers Carter, an ambassador to Afghanistan, brought back to England in 1973 an Afghan hound given to her by Princess Homaira, from a litter born to one of the royal bitches. Chipak, as she grew older, was used to hunt small deer which she killed in the chase. Mrs Carter personally saw the royal dogs used in this manner. It is interesting to note that although they carried a variety of coat patterns the most favoured ones were the lesser, smoother coats which would obviously be far easier to maintain than the heavier ones on a hunting hound. Her own bitch is one of the smoother-coated type which she refused to change when offered an alternative with a heavier coat.

At this present time there are three types of Afghan recognised as such in that country. The most heavily coated is known as Maidorose but in Afghanistan even this type's coat is still not as long as in the Western world. The second type is known as Lochak and has light feathering as opposed to a heavier coat pattern. Lastly there is the type known as Kalogh, which is very sparsely coated and is the most generally found.

The Afghan in Britain

There have been two distinct types of Afghan brought into the country. The racy, slight coated type later known as the Bell Murray Afghan after the family which imported them, and the stockier more heavily coated type, known as the Ghazni's. The Bell Murrays were tall, more delicately built hounds with an underlying steely strength. They were a graceful hound with long necks, longer, more delicately chiselled heads with the triangular eye embodying an aloof expression which was apparently quite beautiful. They were slightly longer cast than their Ghazni counterpart with very well laid shoulders and the foreleg set slightly forward rather than under the shoulder, while the hindquarters were held further back. Their coat was also lighter in its distribution than was the case for the others.

The Ghazni hounds were supposedly from the colder, more mountainous regions and were a smaller, more compact dog altogether, sturdier boned, shorter in the loin and having more spring to their rib. The head carriage was more upright and the whole head was of a slightly stronger type. The fore- and hindquarters were more strongly angulated and were placed more underneath the hound. The eyes were much more forward looking and not as oriental in expression as the more impersonal gaze of the Bell Murrays.

In their own land, from time unknown, we hear of them fulfilling functions as guard dogs, hunters and sheep dogs. In the last case I am sure that there is a very definite instinct of herding since I shall never forget the sight of a brother and sister that I owned many years ago joyously rounding up a herd of bullocks, driving them towards me in the manner of excited children giving a birthday present, only to take them away across a field and then return them once more. This went on for at least half an hour while the village policeman on seeing that I was powerless to stop them sat beside me on the fence until they tired of their game. Never have I seen any pair of trained sheepdogs perform better.

Several dogs were imported from the 1890s onwards but little of significance occurred until the import of Zardin by Captain Barff in 1905. He made a tremendous impact on the show scene, winning the foreign dog class at the Kennel Club Championship Show in 1907 and being subsequently summoned to the Palace so that he could be seen by Queen Alexandria.

The first Kennel Club standard of the breed was based on Zardin but it is said he left no known progeny.

The next stage in the history of the Afghan came when Major and Mrs Bell Murray brought a team of Afghans to Britain.

Then Major and Mrs Amps brought over a kennel of hounds of the mountain type and founded the famous Ghazni kennels. The well known champion Sirdar of Ghazni was amongst them.

There was considerable friction between the two kennels, each considering that they owned the only correct Afghan type. I quote an extract from Mrs Amps' letter. Obviously if she was accustomed to this type of Afghan it would undoubtedly determine her judgement:

> The texture of this coat is a fine silky wool, which is unlike that of any other dog. The distribution of the coat is another characteristic of the breed. The chest, forelegs and hindquarters are heavily coated with long rope-like cords leaving the saddle smooth with a short and much darker hair, usually coarser in texture. The muzzle is clean and dark and an upstanding topknot of long silky hair crowns the head which has very little stop. The long graceful ears are heavily feathered.
>
> The whole effect is rather that of a wig in the time of Charles 2nd. They have large compact feet, and a thin spare tail carried jauntily upward, terminating in a smaller curve. The bitch is usually smaller and carries less coat than the dog. The expression is kind, intelligent and aloof, and this air of complete aloofness from their surroundings is very noticeable on the show bench. They have charming manners, and are essentially a 'one man' dog. I do not advise anyone to keep Afghan Hounds in kennels. They are used to living with man, and when deprived of his company they are unhappy, half-developed and tend to become disobedient. They are good house dogs, marvellously kind and gentle with children.

Mrs Amps in her correspondence stated that in hot areas of the plains the Afghans used occasionally to outcross their dogs with Saluki bitches to get slightly less profuse coats.

Mrs Carter, who has seen the three types of Afghan already mentioned, told me that occasionally the heavier-coated type was bred to the lighter type with the intention of producing a less profuse coat but did not consider that they were Salukis.

Another extract from Mrs Amps' letter gives an interesting picture of the functions of these hounds and the difficulties of keeping them:

> A constant source of trouble to us in Kabul after purchasing an Afghan Hound was the attempts often made to steal back the dogs; they sometimes succeeded in spite of a ten-foot wall and the armed Afghan

guards at each entrance. This was very difficult to circumvent as the dogs were always hidden away in the previous owner's houses in the high-walled Afghan villages where no European may penetrate.

Times have not really changed. In 1973 I was asked by the owner of an Afghan imported from Afghanistan to certify on a Kennel Club form that it was a genuine specimen of the breed. I happily did so. He was a real Afghan. Elegant, slender, slightly long cast by today's show standards, not heavily coated but as far as I was concerned there stood the 'spit and image' of my dearly loved first hound from the old Pushtikuh kennels. He also had the exact temperament attributed to the type: aloof and not too friendly. Actually he had a remarkable quality described in the standard as 'a certain keen fierceness', rarely found today. His owners, who had only recently returned to the country, stated that there had been frequent attempts to steal him and several times they had only just managed to prevent it.

Gradually in England the two types of hounds blended to produce the mixture of types found today.

The breed first achieved championship status in 1925 and the first certificates were won by Afghans of Bell Murray breeding, and in fact, the first champion Afghan was Buckmal bred by Major Bell Murray and owned by Miss Jean Manson.

Kennel names began to be used and some of the first ones can be found behind so many pedigrees. Cove was taken by Miss Manson, Garrymhor belonged to Mrs Couper who owned Garrymore Souriya; Mrs Drinkwater will go down in Afghan history as the owner of the Geufrons, affix of many champions; Mrs Wood owned the Westmill kennel and several champions.

A familiar figure, though starting many years ago, is Mrs Molly Sharpe of Chaman fame. Probably the most famous of many champions was Taj Akbar of Chaman. In those days her kennels were full of golden dogs but now Mrs Sharpe has a great interest in the blue strains.

Dr Betsy Porter, one of the most dedicated of our breed, who, like Mrs Sharpe, sent stock to America during the war so that valuable blood lines should not be lost, founded the El Kabul kennel.

Throughout the greater part of her life she worked wholeheartedly for the breed and was instrumental in the inauguration of training schemes for judges for which she had campaigned for many years.

Other names of that period which can be found behind our pedigrees include: Westover owned by Miss Marjorie Matthews, a devoted worker for the breed; Turkuman, owned by Juliette de Baraclai Levy, now in Israel; the Jalalabad prefix of Mrs Ide and Pushtikuh owned by Miss Helen Semple. Jalalabad was, of course, particularly noteworthy through Sheila Devitt's Jalalabad Barwala of Carloway.

Breeding was of necessity virtually abandoned during the war years, except for the specific purpose of keeping a blood line of use to the breed. Showing was equally curtailed except for small local shows, but after the war it restarted with renewed vigour.

The first dog to be made up after the war was Ravelly Patrols Ali Bey. Bred by Mrs R. Y. Harrison, he was owned and campaigned by Reg Floyd. The Bletchingley kennels of Mrs Peggy Riley came into being in the 1940s and from it there came many champions both in England and abroad. Probably the most well known were Tajomeer, Zara, Houndsman and Hillsman. Houndsman made a great name for himself in Sweden. Bletchingley Ragman of Scheherezade went to America with Lt Col Wallace Pede where he swiftly became American champion and was instrumental in the founding of the famous Scheherazade Afghans.

Mrs Ida Morton's Netheroyd hounds were equally well known and one dog in particular, Ch Netheroyd Ali Baba, held the record number of challenge certificates (19) for many years until she herself awarded a challenge certificate to Clair Races Rifkas Musqat d'Rar, which gave the coveted record to that bitch. This was at the Northern Afghan Hound Association's first championship show in 1969.

Miss Venn produced many excellent dogs in her kennel, one of the last to be seen in the ring was of course the handsome black and tan, Ch Conygar Janse of Carloway, owned by Mrs Diana Bowller.

Miss Eileen Snelling will always be remembered for the many

cream champions produced at her world-famous Khorrassan kennels, among them the beautiful Cleopatra, Moonrise, Portrait and Ivory. Her dogs were famous for soundness of construction, flowing coats and great temperaments.

Contemporary was Sheila Devitt and the Carloway kennels, who became a legend in the breed and whose kennels will always be remembered for the beautiful stock that emerged. Her first champion was Yussef, sire of Pasha of Carloway, a leading Carloway sire who ended his days in my kennel, and there was also the impressive Ch Waliwog of Carloway. Sadly he left these shores to enrich the kennels of Mr David Roche in Australia with another Carloway champion, Mazari. Altogether sixteen champions bear the kennel name of Carloway, made up in the days when there were fewer challenge certificates to be awarded. Mrs Devitt, who left England for Malta in 1965 has maintained her interest in the breed while living overseas and is an international judge.

Another breeder whose kennel became a household word in the breed was Mrs Marna Dods, who owned the Horningsea kennels until her sudden death at a dog show in 1976. She exported dogs who became champions in Australia, America, Scandinavia and on the Continent. She owned the world-famous champion, Horningsea Khanabad Suvaraj, who achieved the title of dog of the year in 1967. She also boosted the popularity of the brindle dog in Britain by making up Ch Horningsea Tiger's Eye, a brindle of elegance and glamour who was to have an enormous effect on the breeding of future kennels.

Many champions were made up at the Horningsea kennels, including Majid, Sheer Khan and Mustagh Ata, all bearing the Horningsea prefix. Mustagh Ata was exported to America and the last champion to be made up by Mrs Dods was one of his descendants she had recently imported, English Ch and American Ch Huzzah Excelsis of Horningsea.

Mrs Dods also sought to help eradicate hereditary faults in Afghans and her work on the behalf of the breed was quite tremendous, both for the standard which she sought to achieve in her own ethics and breeding, and also in training those concerned with the breed.

The Khanabad kennels of Miss Margaret Niblock were founded in 1946 and she has bred several champions made up both by herself and others. Her stock is widely known throughout the world and she is famous for her delightful colours. Ch Khanabad Whuite Warrior was the first pure-white champion Afghan and another of this colour to have joined the titled ranks is Ch Khanabad Peach Blossom owned by Gloria North. Miss Niblock imported a strain of delicate blues and greys which are being used in an extensive breeding programme to produce most interesting colours. She also is renowned as an indefatigable worker for the breed.

Another well known prefix to appear in the 1940s was Vishnu, owned by Mr and Mrs Harrisson. They produced some most beautiful dogs, the most outstanding being Ch Khanabad Azravi of Vishnu and Ch Jali of Vishnu. Both have devoted an enormous amount of time to the breed and are two of our senior championship judges.

For many years now, the Harrissons, instead of breeding, have enjoyed buying and campaigning dogs from other kennels, most of which have become champions, such as one that I bred, Ch Vishnu Sitara of Jagai. It is both interesting and commendable that they have made a stand against what can be described as gambling by breeding, hoping for a champion and in the process producing yet more little Afghans in an already satiated market.

There are so many other kennels equally well known to breeders who all stand at the top of the tree in quality, but who have not bred or shown so frequently, that it really requires another book to do justice to them.

The Ajman kennels of Miss Patricia Kean and Miss Elizabeth McKenzie produced some exquisite reds and blacks and they owned the American-bred import from Cynthia Madigan's Branwen kennels, Ajman Branwen Kandahar, sire of Ch Horningsea Tiger's Eye. They have worked with scrupulous integrity for the breed. They produced some very lovely black dogs from which my own black line was founded.

From the 1940s on there have been many people who have given a great deal to the breed in many ways with a generous distribution of their painstakingly acquired knowledge and who lecture, and sit on panels in the hope of preserving breed characteristics and type. To mention but a few there have been (and many are still extant) the Hall's Barbille kennels who have specialised in keeping alive the Carloway strain. Ali Hupka and his Barakzais, a knowledgeable judge and lecturer with an almost fanatical reverence for the breed.

The 1950s saw the inception of kennels well known in the breed today. Tarril was started by Mr and Mrs Pollock in 1954. They have maintained a steady influence in the breed, pioneered the silver greys and will be particularly remembered for their black-masked silver Ch Kismati Khan of Tarril, who won the hound group at Crufts in 1966.

Mr and Mrs Ronald Adams of the Badakshan kennels became fascinated by brindles and blacks but have not renounced type for glamour. They bred a champion bitch, Ch Badakshan Rani – and have committed themselves utterly to the breed in their devotion to recording as much as possible about Afghans from the earliest known specimens and in lecturing to the later arrivals.

Others among my contemporaries are Mrs Ruth Hughes of the Kalbikhans, who made up Ch Kalbikhan Ali Bey of Carloway and then went on to breed her own. Diana Bowdler-Townsend whose Moonswift hounds are having a far reaching influence on the breed. She speedily made up her first champion, Conygar Janse of Caroloway, and did extremely well with Ch Moonraker of Moonswift. Barbara Etheridge will be remembered for breeding such notable hounds as Ch Takabbor Tiaga.

Mrs Clair Race, another devotee now sadly passed away, bred, amongst several other champions, Rifka's Musqat d'Rar, who broke all records by winning twenty certificates. Musqat and her litter brother Ch Tabaq d'Rar earned the title in the breed of the Heavenly Twins. In all her showing she was ably assisted by one of the stalwarts of our breed, Miss Gillian Knight, who handled her dogs for a large part of the time. The Rifka's also went into partnership with Sheila Devitt in the importation of Wazir of Desertaire from America, a dog which, although tardy in gaining his title in England, had a considerable effect on the breed.

Still to the fore in breeding superb stock are the Rev David Ford and Miss Helen Barnes of Davlen fame. They have exported widely while Father Ford is also an international judge. Their most outstanding dog to date has probably been Ch Aryana Shalym who, after winning his title here, was exported to Canada, where he has had a far-reaching influence on the breed. Ch Hajuba of Davlen who regrettably died at a remarkably early age was a second outstanding dog.

One of the most well known kennels of recent times has been Bondor, founded by Allan Brooks and Eric Swallow. The glamour of their hounds' huge coats and their showmanship caught the imagination of many people and from here came one of my favourite bitches, Afghan of the year 1965, Ch Bondor Serenade. Her sire was the American import Ch Wazir of Desertaire. Many other people also made up Bondor stock to championship status and they included the Sams's Ch Bondor Azim Khan, John Edmonds's Ch Bondor Sayonara and Paul and Carol Harris's Bondor Dera Ghazi Khan. Altogether the Bondors have produced fourteen champions at home and abroad.

Sq Ldr and Pauline Gibbs began to add Afghans to their Montravia poodle kennel starting with the Carloway stock of Fantasie, Ali Khan and Zynnia, who produced the first Montravia stock and then acquired Montravia Bondor Bolero.

Khinjan Afghans have been widely bred and exported and have champions to their credit both at home and abroad. Ch Khinjan Lorcah is to be found in many pedigrees and they also bred a striking black, Ch Khinjan Black Orchid.

Mr Dennis McCarthy has been well known in the breed since he started showing in 1960. He made up a beautiful Khorrassan bitch, Ch Zaza and then went on to produce his own champions, Tara and Tzara, as well as exporting widely. Ch Tzara of Pooghan made yet another record by winning twenty-one challenge certificates.

One of the leading kennels for some time, contemporary with my own (we even started showing at the same time) is the Amudarya kennels of Mrs Anna Paton. Her most well known winner has been Ch Amudarya Khala, who won a great many hound groups and was best in show several times and finally became

ORIGIN AND DEVELOPMENT

Afghan of the year. She also bred the magnificent golden, Ch Amudarya the Pagan, and has exported widely.

As the years have passed, more and more kennels have had their share of winning. Mrs Barbara Taylor, who has owned the Koolaba kennels Afghans for many years, forged ahead with Koolaba Horningsea Eboni Earl, swiftly followed by Koolaba Tajma Zai, a brindle.

Yet another of this vintage is Mrs Carole Walkden-Sturgeon famous for her Alyshan prefix widely shown not only by herself but many others. Her first champion was Int Ch Alyshan Hassan Shabbah, a widely used sire, closely followed by Alyshan Michele.

The Saringa Afghans are owned by Jenny Dove, who had the distinction of breeding and then owning three champions in one

Miss Jenny Dove's homebred Ch Saringa's Abracadabra. This very impressive brindle was the first to be made Champion out of his litter which produced three other Champions

Ch Sacheverell Sukwala, owned and bred by Miss Monica Booth. At the time of writing he is the record breaking championship winner of all time in the breed, with a current total of twenty-three Championships. His proportions are remarkably sound and he is a good example of a well-balanced dog (*Anne Roslin-Williams*)

litter. First she made up the brindle Ch Saringa's Abracadabra, then, black Ch Saringa's Amira followed by Ch Saringa's Andante.

A kennel that has gone on steadily showing and breeding since 1956 has been the Shanshu kennel of Brian and Betty Clark, who made up their Ch Horningsea Mitanni in 1964 and are now showing his great-grandchildren.

Our latest record-breaking champion Afghan is owned by Miss Monica Booth of the Sacheverell prefix, the smoky-shaded Ch Sacheverell Zukwala. Miss Booth made up her first champion, Safiya of Sacheverell, in 1968 who, when mated to Ch Ghuura Khan of Tarril, produced Zukwala, still currently gaining prizes.

A kennel recently disbanded but with a few excellent specimens taken to Malta with their owner is the Miyasht Kennel of Mrs Ann Andrews who intends to use her dogs with Mrs Sheila Devitt – Gilleneys Carloways. Ann started in the 1960s and campaigned her bitch Ueda of Carloway to her title and then bred Miyasht Empress, owned by Anita Doe, and several overseas champions. She also bred the brindle bitch Ch Miyasht Chare Toqmar owned by the Barlows.

More up-and-coming kennels include the Harcourt-Brown family's Kharrissars, who made up as their first champion Kharrissar Karib Khan, and the Hitches, who bred Ch Zendushkas Dazravi, Mrs Ivy Atkins's Koh-in-Noor kennels founded on Carloway and Jagai, and Mrs Dykes's Mirsamir breeding in Wales.

In fact there are so many Afghans being bred by serious breeders with the interests of the Afghan at heart that it is quite impossible to do justice to even a small proportion.

In Afghanistan

In Afghanistan itself, which ought to be the fountainhead of interest and knowledge of our breed, little is known about Afghans. There is no registration system and their position is similar to that of swans in England – basically they all belong to the king. However, they have now become scattered from the king's kennels by being given to loyal friends for safe keeping. There have never been dog shows and therefore lines and stud dogs – though probably kept in the minds of interested parties – do not exist. When the question of registration for Mrs Carter's Chipak arose, it was necessary to contact members of the court in various parts of the world in order to ascertain the exact names of the forebears. No one knows the exact number of Afghans in Afghanistan. It has been estimated that there are probably only a few hundred but since they are guarded so jealously there may be more than one would expect.

In America

There are now large numbers of Afghan enthusiasts the world over and America has the same overpopulation problem that Britain has. The dog-loving population in America is very enthusiastic and flies from one end of the States to the other to show dogs. The shows are arranged so that there can be a 'dog circuit' – the shows are arranged so that owners can travel from one to another in short 'hops'. They leave home with their dogs for several days but cover the same number of shows that in the UK takes several months.

Much American stock springs from British exports and behind many pedigrees are Westmill, Ghazni and Geufron while Chaman and El Kabul dogs went to America on the outbreak of World War II.

Possibly the best known kennel in America is Mrs Kay Finch's Crown Crest. She started to breed in the 1940s with Felts Thief of Bagdad, sire of the near perfect Felts Allah Baba. She acquired Taejon of Crown Crest in 1950 and he swiftly brought her fame by breaking all records. She then imported a dog from Holland, Ch Ophaal van de Orange Manege, sire of Crown Crest Zardonx, and later Crown Crest Mr Universe, the top winning Afghan with a record-breaking career. From her kennels have come a truly impressive number of American champions.

The Stormhill kennel of Virginia and Sandy Withington is one of the most successful. Residing in California, with a vast amount of champions to their credit, they keep their distinctive stamp of flowing elegance and beautiful colours. Started by Virginia Withington, she has been joined by her daughter Sandy to make a formidable team.

Akaba is yet another well known prefix, owned by Mrs Lois Boardman, famous for dogs of elegance and exotic colours. In England she became most well known for her famous champion Akaba's Top Brass.

USA Ch Crown Crest Taejon, one of the first record breakers from this most famous American kennel. He was a great favourite with his owner Mrs Kay Finch and left his stamp indelibly on her line

Still in California is the Coastwind kennel owned by Michael Dunham and Richard Souza which became known in England through Coastwinds Holyman. Recent winners have included the extremely striking Chs Phobos and Abraxas, and indeed the Coastwinds name is always at the top of the list for winning stock.

Connie Miller who, with Ed Gilbert wrote a most comprehensive book on the breed *The Complete Afghan Hound* has bred the Camri Afghans for many years. She has concerned herself not only with breeding excellent stock but with the breed in its entirety — behaviour, structure, hereditary faults and movement.

In Texas are the Dicmar and Summerwine kennels. Dicmar, owned by Dick and Marcia Stoll, has an impressive record of champions over many years, several of which have gone to the Continent. They have particularly specialised in the delicate blues and silvers with attractive variations, owning amongst them the fabulous champion Tajmir's Gunsmoke of Mecca and his grandson Ch Dicmar's Candlelight. Gunsmoke's daughter, Dicmar's Blue Dhimond, took best opposite sex at the National Specialty and at the Garden in New York.

The Summerwines, owned by Sharon and Monroe Jackson, is a small quality kennel with several champions at home and abroad and their Ch Summerwine's Pisco Punch has been a particularly notable winner, one of the top-twenty dogs for several years, as well as a top producing sire. His own dogs inspired Monroe to make some of the world's most unique Afghan jewellery.

Sunny Shay and the Grandeurs are another of the most well known Afghan establishments in the States. She was one of the first to enjoy colour breeding. Her blue-grey champion, Shirkan of Grandeur, will long be remembered winning the Madison Square Garden show in 1957, and the kennel has gone steadily on producing winning stock. It is interesting to note that one of the first Afghans to put this kennel in the limelight was the English import Turkuman Nissims Laurel.

Now in Texas is a kennel formerly based in California — the Hullabaloo Afghans of Earl and Betty Stites. Particularly noteworthy have been their champions Hullabaloos Gloryland and Hullabaloos Mardi Gras. Betty is also a vociferous champion of our breed, particularly where overbreeding for showing is concerned.

The Scheherezade hounds of Lt Col Wallace Pede were started with stock he took with him from England, mainly from the Bletchingly and Mazuri strains. Bletchingley Ragman soon became an American champion and so did Alibaba of Scheherezade and for many years he continued to breed winning and champion stock, before concentrating on his other interest, judging.

The famed Shangrila kennels are owned by Dr Gerda Kennedy, in Oklahoma, from which comes Ch Shangrila Pharahna Phaedra, the top winning bitch of all time. This kennel has long been renowned for both quality and quantity.

In Canada

Afghans have only been a reasonably prominent breed for about ten years, although the first was registered as long ago as 1935, and are made up from English and American bloodlines.

The first kennel of note was Mrs Matchett's El Myria kennels and was based on the Chaman lines.

In the 1940s came the Holloway's Queensway kennels, based on the Patrols line from England, and their stock is still producing winners.

The 1950s saw the Larade kennels, owned by the Hamptons. Soon after, the Kophi kennels of Dr and Mrs Myles Phillips were founded. They later imported a dog who became Canadian Ch Horningsea Tzaama and then in 1966 they imported from England the well known Ch Aryana Shalym.

Dr Marsh and his wife took the Marchonique kennels to Canada from England and founded a very well known establishment there.

Now the point has come at which a great many Afghans are bred, some seriously, and some, as in other countries, with insufficient concern for the future of the breed, but with thought only of the immediate gain in dollars. It is interesting and heartening to note, however, that only people with at least ten years' experience in the ring and in breeding may judge, as well as having qualifications denoting genuine interest in the breed. This should help maintain high standards.

In Australia

Australia is vast and therefore there are regional kennel clubs in several areas, each with its own rules and under the overall guardianship of the Australian National Kennel Council. The breed began to come into its own on this continent in the 1960s with stock imports from the Carloway, Bletchingley and Khorrassan lines.

Mrs Barbara Skilton took Afghans of both the Bletchingley and Pushtikuh lines back to Australia with her from which she commenced breeding in the 1950s, also using the imported Taj Amigo of Chaman.

As these hounds started to grip the imagination, so dogs from many kennels were imported from Britain as well as the States and Europe.

David Roche of the well known Fermoy kennels imported two particularly beautiful Carloway hounds, Ch Waliwog of Carloway and Ch Mazari of Carloway, both heavily coated impressive goldens. He also imported Khinjan and Pooghan bitches and bred from them until turning his attention toward American lines, notably Crown Crest and then Coastwinds. He is well known in England, particularly for his judging of best in show at Crufts 1969.

Mrs Helen Furber of the leading Furbari kennels bought El Kabul stock from Dr Betsy Porter, which proved to be extremely successful with her Australian-bred stock.

The Schelling's Shaaltarah kennel imported stock from the Chandhara line, Chandhara Wazir Shah, Chandhara's Talukdar and Chandhara's Tarkuhn Khan, as well as Horningsea Kishta.

Graham Paulchen and Lyle Dally also imported Chandhara breeding with considerable success. Wendy and Stuart Slatyer imported both English and American breeding for their Calahorra kennel. They have done particularly well with their home-bred champions Mustapha and Mosque.

Australian Ch Furbari Ulysses, owned by Mrs C. Kelly and bred by Mrs Helen Furber, was National Dog of the year in Australia in 1974

There are now imports from most of the major British kennels in Australia. They include Horningsea, Moonswift, Jagai, Shanshu, Davlen, as well as the Dutch Orange Manege, all adding much impetus to the Afghan scene, while Dr Newbury, who took back Bondor Maskencostum from England, concentrates on the existing Carloway blood lines with other English stock.

In New Zealand

This country runs parallel to a certain extent through interchange of animals with Australia.

Stock has also been imported from England from Conygar Janze; from the Miyasht line; the Moonswift kennel and dogs of Carloway, Horningsea and Bletchingley breeding as well as from the Shanshu dogs. The leading kennels have been Mr Tait's Tholae, where several champions have been bred; Mr Walker's Reklaw strain and the Taff kennel name of Mrs Morris are equally well known.

In South Africa

Breeding takes place on a comparatively smaller scale in this country, but the kennel owners are proving themselves to be most dedicated. Originally there was stock from American and Continental kennels, but of late some excellent British breeding has been taken out from the UK by British breeders who have emigrated, as well as the established South Africans importing dogs from this country. Breeders include Mr and Mrs Gainsborough of the Cathcart kennels, Mrs June Bracey, and Mrs James of the Shirekhan Afghans.

In Scandinavia

This country has some most beautiful hounds of both English and American breeding with Orange Manege intermixed.

For many years Mrs Ingrid af Trolle was owner of one of the foremost kennels. It started with the Belgian-born Int Ch Baghdad R'Akela and then she imported a dog sired by Amanullah Khan of Acklam from a Chaman bitch from Belgium to found the El Kandahar kennel, which has produced many champions.

One of the most famous Scandinavian imports of all time, which proved to have a far-reaching influence on the breed, was Int Ch Xenos van de Orange Manege from Eta Pauptit's kennel in Holland, particularly by producing a great sire for the Tajmahal kennels, and also Int Ch Tanjores Domino, a stud force in America. Bletchingley Houndsman arrived from England and was a most prolific sire of champions both for the Kandahar and Ismail kennels before his untimely death in a fire destroyed Mrs af Trolles' kennels.

Sweden has also imported many dogs who have become champions in the last decade. Khinjan Baryak did extremely well and

Haboob of Katwiga is an International and German Champion, who in 1974 became the first German-bred Afghan to win the Dutch Championship

Miss Birgitta Runmarker imported Swedish Ch Moonta of Carloway and Finnish and Swedish Ch Pussy Willow of Jagai, whom she later used successfully as a brood bitch.

Finland has of recent years come well to the fore with some magnificent dogs bred from stock imported from Sweden and England with lines that include the Bletchingley from an import sired by American Ch Bletchingley Ragman and Int Ch Tajmahal Abdul Djari. The leading kennels have been Tiohi-Tikan and Mazar-I-Sharif.

Denmark has as its leading kennel the El Kamas, whose importation of Horningsea-bred stock, Ch Horningsea Shikari and Ch Horningsea Jamusah has produced outstanding dogs. A later import included the brindle bitch Ch Badakshan Tigran, a daughter of Ch Horningsea Tiger's Eye.

The American import Int Ch Panameric of Stormhill had a far-reaching effect on Afghans throughout Scandinavia, since he has been widely used and more and more breeders have mingled the American blood in one of the last strongholds of the older British and Continental lines.

In Germany

One immediately thinks of the El Kairas prefix of Herr Frankenburger and Mrs Erika Rodde's Katwiga Afghans. The German dogs have been most strongly influenced by the Van de Orange Manege lines, dogs bred in Holland by Eta Pauptit, which have consistently remained true to the Ghazni stock from which they were founded.

Herr Frankenburger's first dog was of Acklam and Chaman stock through the VDOM breeding. He also imported from England Matatina of Moonswift, which he used in his lines with great success, subsequently importing blue breeding through Branwen Kazar. He then concentrated on producing blues and blacks with some delicate greys. The imported Matatina of Moonswift was used to effect with VDOM breeding to found a line of reds which he has carefully kept separate from the blues and has therefore managed to keep two excellent types. Also imported to the El

ORIGIN AND DEVELOPMENT

Kairas kennel was stock from the Pandjah kennel of Madame Fosse in Belgium and he finally bred the first silver blue in Germany. From these lines several champions resulted, when Ch Europa El Kaira was mated to Branwen Sheen Taufaar. Later imports from England included blue Kabella puppies and Khanabad True Blue, and now he concentrates on breeding these beautiful colours.

Mrs Roddes kennel has remained exclusively the stronghold of VDOM breeding and she still keeps the pure Ghazni type, starting originally with a daughter of Ch Nabob VDOM. She became a champion and was bred to Ch Vladimir VDOM. Mrs Rodde now has what is virtually the purest of that line – since Eta Pauptit gave up her kennels – and she possesses several champions.

One of the Champions from Herr Frankenburger's kennel in Germany, Miss Mandy El Kaira is a sample of excellent and careful breeding for sound structure with a pleasing coat

In Belgium

The Pandjah kennels of M and Madame Fosse are well to the fore with dedicated breeders importing to improve stock when they feel it necessary.

In France

The position at the moment is not entirely settled. Stock has been introduced from England and the States and there is a great deal of enthusiasm and also quite a large Afghan population.

In Switzerland

There is a great deal of interest in the breed and basically Dutch and German lines, with a great concentration on breeding winning stock. M Rigouleau's Chandigarh kennel is beginning to make quite a name for itself.

In Iberia

Here the first Afghans were brought in by Mrs Schultz in the 1940s and were of Swedish origin. In the 1950s stock was introduced from India bred by the Maharajah of Baria from dogs sent to India from England from the Khorrassan and Bletchingly kennels.

In the 1960s Cynthia Madigan from the United States made an enormous impact with Afghans from the Grandeur line which included Ch Diablo of Grandeur, and they have played a significant part in Spanish, Continental and English breeding. From these kennels the blue dogs Branwen Sheen Khalifa and Branwen Sheen Kurram were imported to England by Margaret Niblock; and Ajman Branwen Kandahar, a black brindle, arrived and sired Ch Horningsea Tiger's Eye and is now to be found in a great many

Facing page
Ch Bondor Dera Ghazi Khan with Carol Harris, co-owner with her husband Paul, proving that a show champion has as much energy and as great a need for exercise as any working dog

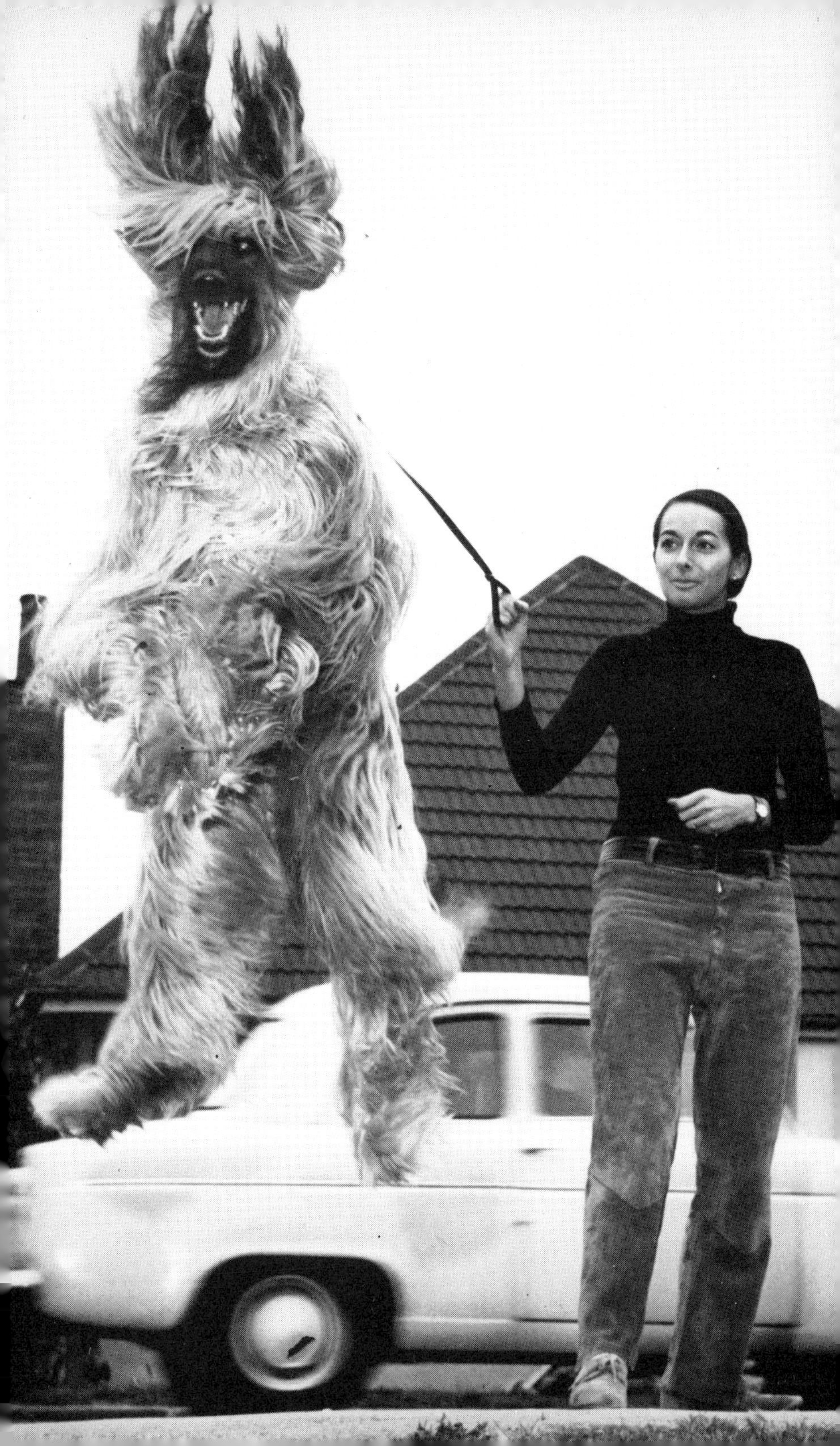

British pedigrees. It was also from this kennel that Miss Hunt-Crowley imported Branwen Sheen Camri.

In 1971 Mr Norman Huidabro brought Afghans of American origin from Chile, including Ch Antar Rakashi and Huilacos Zolah, both of which became Spanish and Portuguese champions. Rakashi distinguished himself through becoming Int and Monagesque Ch. Mr Huidobro also brought a black bitch, Ch Huilacos Akaba Diddi, who is a producer of many champions. He has continued to import stock from Chile and has won a great many top awards with his champions, and has bred a great many winners of top awards.

Other top kennels include Mr Antonio Rosados Corregidor hounds; he owns Spanish and Portuguese Ch Saringas Cadilesker, Khanabad Rett Kundar and Faiazabad.

In Portugal little breeding is done and the main kennel belongs to Miss Carla Molinari, bearing the name of Vale Negro. She owned the famous English, Portuguese and Int Ch Takabbor Tiaga, a multiple best-in-show winner, and imported from America Ch Dicmar's Silver Satin, and American, Portugese and Canadian Ch Gini's E. Magnus Rex of Foxrun. She has based her breeding on Horningsea lines with the addition of the American Grandeur, Akaba, Crown Crest and Stormhill lines.

In Ireland

So near to England and mainly started by British stock are the Irish kennels. In fact the first Afghan was registered with the Irish Kennel Club in 1927 and was bred by Miss Jean Manson (Kibi of Cove). D. J. Cronin founded the Enriallac kennels and some of these dogs are behind our English pedigrees.

It is interesting to note that in a show catalogue of 1937 two familiar names occur that are in the ring with us today, Mrs Molly Sharpe of the Chamans and Mr Bill Kelly of the Sherdils, both exhibiting in Ireland. To this day there is a constant stream of British exhibitors to the Irish championship shows.

In 1946 an Irish dog, O'Toole's Vendas Tash Down, was best of breed at Crufts.

ORIGIN AND DEVELOPMENT

The top award in Ireland under the Irish Kennel Club rules is called a green star. These are valued on a points system, which takes into account both entries at the show and also the number of IKC registration. Dogs are Irish champions only; they have to win at English shows to become an English champion.

The major breeders are Mr Bob Margrain of the Arkenstone prefix, best known for his top-winning Irish champions, Arkenstone Mythewraithe and Arkenstone Apollo. A most serious and dedicated breeder, he is endeavouring to maintain two lines, both stemming from Horningsea Majid. He started his kennels with a Sherdil-bred dog and has also imported a son of the brindle, Ch Sherrendale Brandy. The Metewand kennel of Anne Mathers

Irish Ch Arkenstone Apollo, one of Ireland's top dogs, bred and owned by Mr Robert Margrain; Apollo is sired by Ch Moonraker of Moonswift

started in 1970; she has now established a line of elegant blacks. Her first dogs came from the Arkenstone kennels and she made up the Irish champion, Arkenstone Pink Panther.

The Beares of Dublin run the Nilbud kennels with some impressive winners. Marjorie and Colette Doody and the Yazdan kennels are firmly established and are well known throughout Ireland for their devotion to the breed.

For some years the Moonswift Afghans were based in Ireland and their influence can be felt throughout Irish stock. Mrs Borst of the Veldspringer Afghans made up Mandarin of Moonswift to Irish champion. She also took to Ireland from England the Dutch-bred black dog, Veldspringer Engelandvaader van de Emelenburg, litter brother to my own Kuzanda van de Emelenburg of Jagai, the dam of Ch Begum Kanda of Jagai.

In 1967 there appeared to be only about a dozen people in Ireland with Afghans but now there are flourishing breed clubs and regular breed shows of both open and championship status, thanks to a small band of hardworking enthusiasts.

It has been impossible to mention all the kennels and dogs and Afghan folk that I would have wished, but I have tried to give an overall picture of the state of the breed as far as possible. Where we go in the future depends on the integrity of future breeders and whether they wish to preserve our hound in all his strength and dignity or whether he is going to degenerate as a result of show ambition.

10
Breed Clubs and Afghan Standard

Breed clubs

Breed clubs have been formed in various regions to fulfil two definite needs: to promote the interests and welfare of the breed; to concentrate particularly on an allotted area. Parent club of them all is the Afghan Hound Association, the largest breed and the supposedly national club. I say 'supposedly' only because most clubs find that they have members from all the areas in large or smaller quantities who join to obtain the club's magazine, or because they get a free insurance with membership, or some similar reason. Most Afghan folk belong to at least two clubs. I actually belong to five and have a nodding acquaintance with the others. The Afghan Hound Association makes no claim to concentrate on any single area but covers them all and holds its shows in an assortment of venues all over England.

The main aim is of course to further the interests of the breed and to promote the adherence to the breed standard, and to this end the clubs run shows, endeavour to help newcomers with their dogs, and train aspiring judges, as well as help with unwanted and unfortunate dogs.

The shows are usually the most publicised features of the societies and in all probability they will run three of them a year. Most of the breed clubs now run a championship show, where, hopefully, the cream of Afghans should be seen. They are run by the committees of these societies who give hours and even days to running the clubs.

Ch Azravi of Vishnu, owned by Mr and Mrs Charles Harrison. An impressively-built dog of great character, his soundness is shown in the easy stance of his hindquarters, the strong topline and the chiselling of the foreface with strong lower jaw (*P. J. Sanger*)

These shows promote the interest of the breed through enabling dogs of a certain standard to win, to be seen, and also for the breed fanciers to get together with, it is sincerely hoped, advantages to all. Indirectly they assist in training future judges, since they can learn by example and also develop their own critical faculties.

For those genuinely interested in the background of the breed there is often the exciting event of a parade of champions, in which titled hounds of all ages and both sexes parade before the assembled company, reliving for a few moments their past glories and revelling in the applause as they make their circuit. Indeed it is a heart-warming sight to see the years drop away as they face their audience. The Southern Afghan Club and the Afghan Hound Association have run particularly successful events.

For many years it has been felt by responsible people with the interest of the breed at heart that it has been too easy to become a judge. In many cases it has been merely a matter of knowing someone who could help, and we have watched in wonder at the odd friendships and alliances formed through a newcomer going all out to further his own interests but without considering the dogs' interests, and with no thought for the future with which he will (if he lasts in the breed) be undoubtedly involved.

The clubs have therefore evolved qualifications through which newcomers should make their approach to judging, under rules first formulated by the clubs and then discussed by the breed council which was formed from representatives of the clubs. The rules make it necessary that a particular number of years of active participation in the breed should have passed before a candidate can take his junior judge's exam and so be put on a breed club's list and start his career.

Unfortunately, as this is not upheld by the Kennel Club, any inexperienced folk may still judge the breed without qualifying in any way.

The training schemes followed by most of the breed clubs follow a similar pattern. The trainees are given lectures in conformation which will help them to understand the structure of the dog, how and why it moves in a particular manner and how they can breed to prevent excessive exaggeration with its subsequent crippling faults – in fact, why the breed is built in its own particular manner to fulfil its own particular function.

There are also lectures about the Afghan with relation to the breed standard, the ethics of judging and the art of managing a ring. Finally there is practical instruction on handling the dog in the ring and assessing the points of an exhibit.

Another of the most important activities encountered in the breed clubs is their work on behalf of all the unfortunate Afghans

Afghans are not invariably sleek, well-groomed status symbols, they revel in mud – the wetter the better (*Chris Hill*)

who are neglected, ill-treated or just plain unwanted. This work is run under the title of 'Rescue Schemes' and every area club has its own representative responsible for finding homes for the unwanted ones and organising care and sometimes veterinary treatment for the ones in very bad condition.

An increasing number of Afghans have become unwanted, thanks to the population explosion which has rocketed Kennel Club registrations sky high. I need in fact only to quote the experience of one rescue officer, Mr Hitch of the Southern Afghan Club, to give a picture of the results of indiscriminate breeding.

Mr Hitch found that the main reasons for many of our rescue cases has been the 'pin-money pirates'. They breed just to sell to dealers, who take the litter at a very early age for quite reasonable prices, when one considers how little effort, thought or good things have been put into the puppies. They are then sold quickly with no help or information, or after-sales help.

Then come the local councils who refuse to allow dogs to be kept in council houses. Naturally a dog's owner is reluctant to pass over the possibility of a better house. Once more the breeder is at fault in having in the first place sold a puppy to such a person. It is incumbent upon every breeder to make sure that anyone wishing to purchase a dog is living in the right environment and circumstances to be able to give it the life it should be able to expect as a birthright.

Other unwanted dogs come as a result of broken homes, death, divorce, imprisonment, the unwanted Christmas present, and occasionally we are asked to find a home when someone is leaving the country.

The rescue officer has the unenviable task of arranging for collection, delivery and temporary accommodation which sometimes takes the form of kennelling or sometimes of being looked after by a kind-hearted committee member. Then he has to match the dog to a suitable home, depending on upbringing, history, and present circumstances. Very rarely does he take the dog to a second owner as much thought and research goes into finding new homes.

In 1974 the Southern Afghan Club alone had 125 dogs through their hands. In 1975 there were 105 and the first eight months of 1976 produced about 85 rescue cases.

The only complaint received from new owners is that they are refused the pedigrees of the dogs (where known), therefore they cannot compare the merits of their Afghan with others they meet. However our ruling is that we refuse to give pedigrees, as we do not wish these unfortunate dogs, who have probably already had very hard lives, to be exploited as cheap puppy factories or to be the easy beginnings to a kennel.

In order to combat the practise of buying an Afghan without adequate preparation, all club officers will give hours of their time explaining the difficulties and problems that could lie ahead of any unwary purchaser, and we do our best to answer the myriad questions which we are asked at all hours of the night.

Apart from these aspects of a club's function there is a lighter side: the social occasions; the magazines; the racing where the Afghan owners 'go to the dogs'.

BREED CLUBS AND AFGHAN STANDARD

This sport was started because many people felt that there was a need for more free running for Afghans kept in flats and houses with small gardens.

The first meetings, run by the Afghan Hound Association, took place at Northdown Greyhound track at Blindley Heath, Surrey. One of the first to do well was the elegant Ch Ranjitsinjhi of Jagai, and various others of the titled fraternity to gain their stars were Ch Amudaraya the Pagan, Ch Amudarya Khala and Ch Alyshan Hassan Shabbah.

The meetings take place on Sunday afternoons between May and August, at several tracks in England and Wales.

Both pet owners and show dogs participate and it has become a most happy social occasion. Mr John Callow, the racing organiser, who was the inaugurator, has said many times how rewarding it is to see rescue Afghans participating in this event with their new owners.

Afghans at a race meeting. Note the light muzzles and the racing silks on dogs obviously enjoying every minute of the dash round the track (*Syndication International*)

BREED CLUBS AND AFGHAN STANDARD

The distances which Afghans have run progressed from the shortish course of 280yd, through the distances of 400yd, 580yd, to 700yd and on to 1,175yd.

Most breed clubs run a magazine of some description. The Southern Afghan club runs a really informative one three times a year which is distributed free to members. Once more, dedicated people in the form of Paul and Carol Harris of the Ghaziris Afghans spend weeks on the production of each edition and articles are wheedled out of correspondents all over the world. Such publications also run advertisements for kennels about puppies and stud dogs as well as giving practical information on various aspects of dog care.

The AHA gives a free third-party insurance to each paid-up member of the club instead of such regular publications and issues a newsletter.

Finally there is the social side of the breed clubs. Each holds at least one function at which the members are able to meet in non-doggy clothes, leave the lead and its other end behind and have a friendly meal and chat. The strange thing is that even here, when everyone is turned out in gala rig, what do they talk about? Afghans.

Before discussing the standard which every breed club works so hard to uphold, here is part of an article in the US magazine *Showcase* by Betty Stites of the Hullabaloo Afghans. It airs similar thoughts to ones uppermost in many of our minds today.

> To me it seems that the Afghan can survive in its true form only if we as breeders and exhibitors remember that this breed originated to serve a purpose. Originally, of course, he was a hunter. He needed a balanced, powerful body with good strong bone for endurance. He needed large, thick padded feet. He needed depth of brisket and spring of rib to give him the lung capacity demanded of a runner. He needed keen eyes to sight game. He needed angulation of shoulder and rear to enable him to run and move correctly. This combined with his pelvic assembly enabled him to maneuver. He needed coat of some sort to cope with the tremendous temperature changes experienced in the deserts and hills of Afghanistan. He also needed a keen and composed mental attitude. He had to be an independent thinker, able to make his

own decisions without command from a higher authority. He needed a calm, quiet, serenity, a totally unflappable outlook so he could sit back and survey the entire situation before coming to a decision as to what to do about it. Indeed, he was a king, both mentally and physically.

And what have we made of this marvelous animal? In some cases it's sad to contemplate, and sadder still when it's viewed in the ring. How can we condone the whispy little creatures we see in the ring, with barely enough bone to allow them to stand, and often scarcely the muscle tone needed for any kind of movement. How can we condone the extreme over refinement of head, lacking both power and brain space, with little or no underjaw. Such an animal could never in its wildest dreams bring down and kill an animal, and undoubtedly wouldn't even stand a chance of catching it. How can we condone the unsound movement, legs flipping here and there, the amazing lack of reach, due in many cases to overly straight shoulders, and the almost complete loss of the correct springy movement? How can we condone the shallow, weedy bodies with little or no brisket and lung capacity. How can we condone the long, soft, floppy backs, scarcely serving any purpose.

What of our temperament? Where is the fierce, cold eyed independence? Where is the keen independent thinker, who knew no master but himself? Sadly, all but gone. We now have a race of soft eyed, waggy tailed, vacant minded, unthinking atomatons.

We have done this to our breed, and in some cases it would seem we have done it on purpose. We, as breeders, have made our breed what it is today, and in all too many cases, that seems to be simply an unsound coat carrier, soft of mind and muscle, who is able only to go into a ring, wag his tail, dance about, and win. Who in the breed can really believe that all we want is a hairy, prancing crowd pleaser? If this is the case, it would seem we might better have considered another breed.

The standard of the Afghan hound

Characteristics
The Afghan hound should be dignified and aloof with a certain keen fierceness. The Eastern or Oriental expression is typical of the breed. The Afghan looks at and through one.

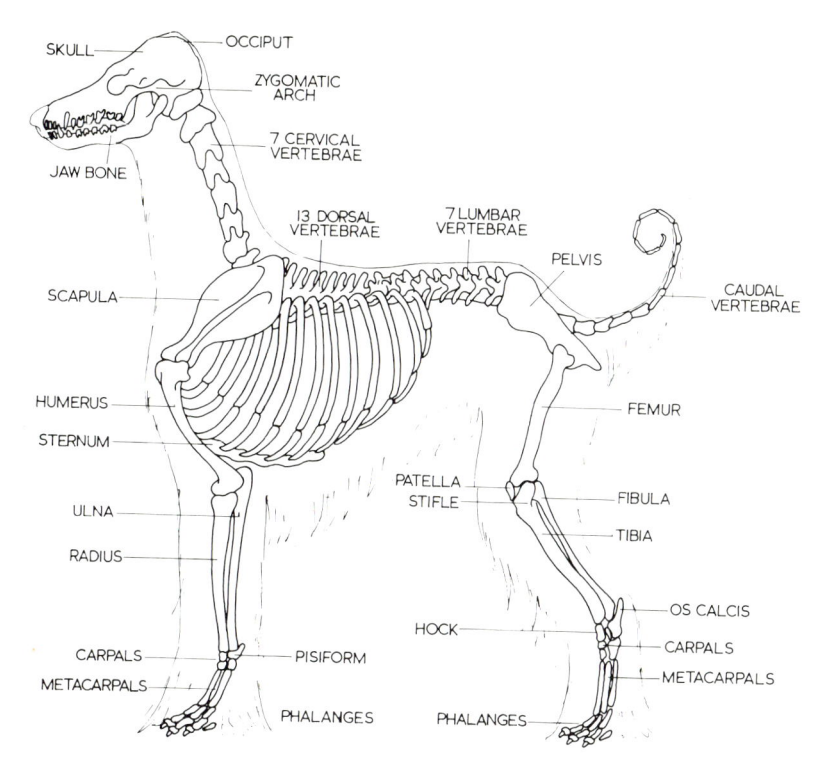

General appearance
The gait of the Afghan hound should be smooth and springy with a style of high order. The whole appearance of the dog should give the impression of strength and dignity combining speed and power. The head must be held proudly.

Head and skull
Skull long, not too narrow with prominent occiput. Foreface long with punishing jaws and slight stop. The skull well balanced and surmounted by a long 'top-knot'. Nose preferably black but liver is not debarred in light-coloured dogs.

Eyes
Should be dark for preference but golden colour is not debarred. Nearly triangular, slanting slightly upwards from the inner corner to the outer.

Ears
Set low and well back, carried close to the head. Covered with long silky hair.

Mouth
Level.

Neck
Long, strong with proud carriage of the head.

Forequarters
Shoulders long and sloping, well set back, well muscled and strong without being loaded. Forelegs straight and well boned, straight with shoulder, elbows held in.

Body
Back level, moderate length, well muscled, the back falling slightly away to the stern. Loin straight, broad and rather short. Hip-bones rather prominent and wide apart. A fair spring of the ribs and good depth of chest.

Hindquarters
Powerful, well bent and well turned stifles. Great length between hip and hock with a comparatively short distance between hock and foot. The dew claws may be removed or remain at the discretion of the breeder.

Feet
Forefeet strong and very large both in length and breadth and covered with long thick hair, toes arched. Pasterns long and springy, especially in front and pads well down on the ground. Hindfeet long, but not quite so broad as forefeet, covered with long thick hair.

Tail
Not too short. Set on low with ring at the end. Raised when in action. Sparsely feathered.

Coat
Long and very fine in texture on ribs, fore- and hindquarters and flanks. From the shoulder backwards and along the saddle the hair should be short and close in mature dogs. Hair long from the forehead backward, with a distinct silky 'top-knot'. On the foreface the hair is short as on the back. Ears and legs well coated. Pasterns can be bare. Coat must be allowed to develop naturally.

Colour
All colours are acceptable.

Weight and size
Ideal height: Dogs 68.5cm to 73.5cm. Bitches 5.08cm to 7.5cm smaller. Ideal weight: Dogs 27.2kg to 29.5kg. Bitches 2.3kg less.

Faults
Any appearance of coarseness. Skull too wide and foreface too short. Weak underjaw. Large round or full eyes. Neck should never be too short or thick. Back too long or too short.

Note
Male animals should have two apparently normal testicles fully descended into the scrotum.

There is room for quite considerable latitude in the interpretation of the standard, according to personal preferences, but one can evolve rules of thumb about what should be found.

Characteristics
These dogs are by nature proud and intelligent with an aloof and often haughty bearing, but aloofness should not be confused with nerves which prevent a dog from being handled, nor should viciousness be confused with that 'certain keen fierceness'. This latter quality has seemed to me, since seeing some Afghans from their native country, quite indescribable but impossible to mistake when once one sees it . . . Afghans must not look too gentle and too kind, adorable though some of their expressions may be.

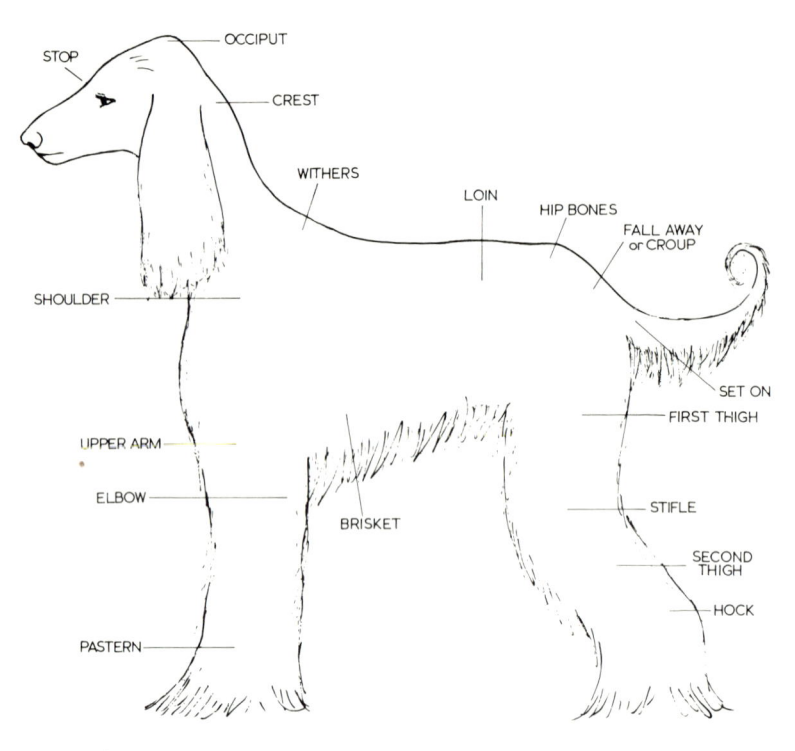

General appearance

We start with an anomaly. Smooth and springy. Two terms which cancel each other out. However, one can look for a lightness in the gait that can only be produced by a superbly muscled animal. The feet are not thrust down heavily with a flat-footed paddling motion. There should be the impression of a coiled spring in action. In his general gait he is a joyful dog with a superb head carriage enhanced by the fact that he uses his eyes, which immediately causes the head to lift. He does not follow a scent unless a particularly attractive bitch has walked there before him. Obviously the style of high order does not allow hocks to knock, front legs to 'come out of one hole', hind feet to overshoot the front feet or for any foot to be thrown out in any direction. Nor does it allow for the hackney action which is so often mistakenly admired by the novice, of the trotting horse, where the forepaws lift practically to the level of the chin.

The head and skull can be worked out to a fairly simple proportion if the length of the skull from the occiput to the stop is equal to the length from the stop to the tip of the nose. Seen from the side that is a balanced skull. Seen from above or directly facing, the skull must not be too wide or round and there should not be much more than the length of an eye between the two eyes themselves.

Remembering that this is a hunting hound, it follows that a snipey head is incorrect. The punishing jaw should have a definite and clearly defined underjaw and be capable of biting and killing its prey. The lower jaw should not be so shelly as to be invisible beneath a fold of the upper lip when the mouth is closed.

Over-refinement, with subsequent loss of bite, malformation of the teeth, and in some cases lack of teeth is unacceptable.

A head without a stop, Borzoi style is equally incorrect, however refined and elegant it may appear to be. Although there is no actual statement in the standard that the nose must be 'Roman' it is accepted that this slight downward curve just behind the nose is correct. Indeed it is found in the greater proportion of Afghans. The straighter, almost turned-up nose (dish face), is not acceptable.

Afghan lips are neat and firm, they do not hang pendulously, nor are they loose at the corners.

Eyes
This is the source of the Afghan expression. If the eye is round or too full the oriental expression is immediately lost, but it is enhanced by the triangular shape and the exotic upward tilt at the outer corner, particularly if there is very definite 'eye lining'. In the US standard the eye is described as almond and the dogs have a gentle softening of expression due to the round delicate curve of the lid. We also have this in a few dogs owing to the background of US-bred stock in our lines. Although the standard states that a golden colour is not debarred, nevertheless it is not at all pleasing in a very dark face. In a selfmask, a colour that blends in neatly with the mask is quite acceptable. No mention is made of pink haws in the standard, a thickening and lightening in colour of the membrane in the inner corner of the eye, but there is no doubt that it

ruins expression and shape and in my opinion should be penalised, particularly as it tends to be a hereditary fault.

Ears
As a general rule a satisfactory ear placement is achieved when the ear grows from a position level with the outer corner of the eye. The leathers should be long, reaching well past the jaw bone and covered with long silky hair. One wonders, however, whether the hair that grows well past the shoulder in some Afghans is really compatible with a dog basically evolved for hunting.

Mouth
There are two types of acceptable bite – level and scissors. A level bite is found in the minority of dogs. The top and bottom teeth actually meet with the biting edges touching. The usual bite, of which there is no mention in the standard, but which is generally considered correct for the Afghan, is the scissor bite. This bite, which is the most useful and the most functional, has the upper incisors sliding neatly over the lower teeth without any undue gap between. An undershot jaw is quite incorrect and is dangerous to accept in any dog that may be used for stud, since this condition is hereditary. A wry mouth, in which one side may be undershot and the other overshot, so twisted can it become, can be hereditary, although very rarely it can be caused by an early accident. I once had a puppy break its jaw bone neatly down the centre during a very difficult birth and subsequent hand feeding. The precise moment at which it occurred I never knew. The break was found by an orthodontic specialist later in life when I had it examined under anaesthetic since I could not understand that condition in this particular line. (He was even able to pinpoint the approximate time at which it must have been done.)

Neck
A long neck is most desirable since it balances the rest of the dog and nothing looks worse than a magnificently built hound with its head too near its shoulders. The strong, well muscled neck is slightly arched as in a horse. It is in the Ghazni type of hound very

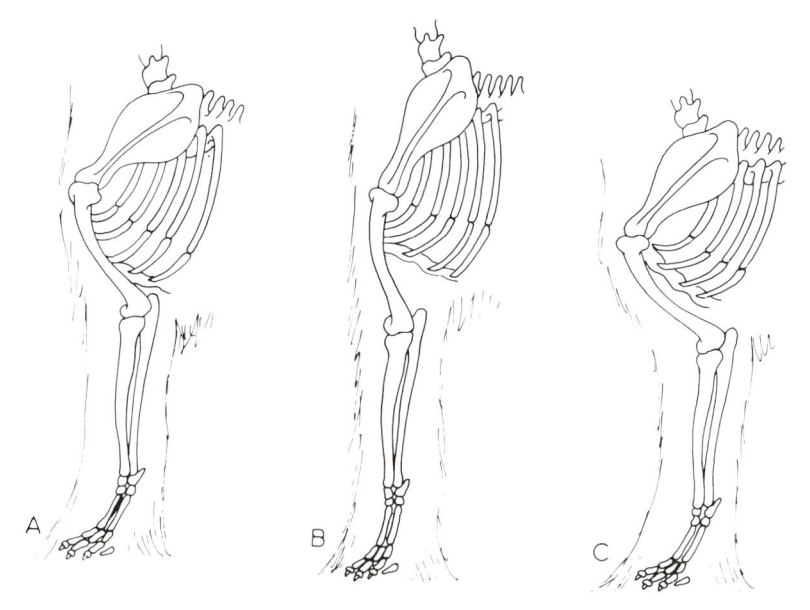

Forequarters: **A** has the correct shoulder angulation; **B** shows a completely straight shoulder and upright pastern; **C** has a rather upright shoulder with a compensating over-angulation of the upper arm placing the foreleg too far under the body

upright with the head balanced proudly on top. A hanging neck is a sad sight on any Afghan and gives a dreary effect, since the muscles from the neck no longer pull up the forelegs so smartly. In the Bell Murray type which is still seen as a basis in some dogs, despite the mixtures perpetrated in the name of breeding, the neck has a forward direction but it is still strong and powerful with a nicely poised head.

Forequarters
In a well laid shoulder the scapula is, ideally, at an angle of 45° to the ground. It also slopes gently inward at the top to give a width of not more than 2in at the most between them. They must not be too close since they would obviously draw nearer together as the neck is thrust forwards and so impede movement (see illustration).

The upper arm or humerus is set onto the scapula at an angle of approximately 90°. This gives a good shoulder angulation with the forelegs set well under the dog in line with the top of the shoulder.

The foreleg is straight and on no account must the elbows slope outward or inward. As a rule it should be possible to place some three or four fingers between the forelegs at the top touching the sternum.

If there is insufficient width there is the weak appearance of 'two pins out of one hole' or an 'A line' in movement. Too much width will cause the elbows to protrude and the feet may have a tendency to turn in or out. A common fault is to find the front feet 'plaiting' in movement. The elbows must neither be pushed outward or turned sharply inwards, although they should be held in firmly at the shoulder.

Body
'Moderate length' is rather ambiguous. It gives no actual proportion but it is usually accepted that a dog is relatively square with the length from the front to the base of the tail equal to the height from the floor to the top of the shoulder. The back therefore will be proportionate. There should not be a steep slope from the top of the shoulder directly down to the tail without any fall-away or hip bones. Rather the back should be comparatively level, although there is often a slight muscular pad on the loin of an active well muscled hound. The loin should not be wispy and muscle must not be sacrificed to elegance. The hip bones should be prominent, even though the dog is not bony or emaciated, and there should be a fall-away of reasonable length at an angle to the ground. This fall-away, or croup, is formed by the hip bones.

The ribs should, of course, have a fair spring but they should not barrel out too widely since this impedes the movement of the elbow and causes them to thrust outwards, so ruining the frontal movement (see illustration). If they are narrow in section or 'slab-sided' there is insufficient room for the lungs and heart of what is, or should be, basically a hunting hound. As a general rule, when assessing the depth of the loin, the sternum should be on a level with the elbow of the dog.

The ideal shape, sectionally, of the rib cage, is of an inverted pear which gives adequate room for the essential organs but also allows for the easy movement of the elbow.

There are two terms in common dog parlance 'long cast' and 'short coupled'. The long-cast dog has a body long in proportion and it can be made up in two ways – a normal length of rib with a longer loin or a long rib cage with a normal loin. In a short-coupled dog, which is a feature found desirable by many in the show ring, there is often a very short loin but once more the dog can have a normal loin with a variation in the length of the rib cage, in this case a much shorter one.

The short-coupled dog may not move so well as it may have to take a shorter stride to avoid the back legs hitting the front ones. In a hunting dog I feel that this 'smart' shape would be totally unacceptable. The long-cast dog is frequently a very sound mover but if the muscling is poor then there could be a tendency to a dippy back or a swing to the hips.

Hindquarters
These are a most characteristic feature of the Afghan, combining strength with grace. There is a long lower thigh with a slightly shorter upper thigh bone and a well angulated stifle joint. If the length of the fibia and femur is too even then there can be a weak 'kneeling' appearance when the dog is stacked. The standard calls for a well bent stifle but it does not at any point indicate anything approaching overangulation, a cause of weakness and poor hind movement. An angle of 125° to 130° is quite adequate and will retain strength to produce the powerful thrust that propels the dog forward (see illustration). Proportionately the length between the hock to the foot is very short in comparison to the length from the hip join to the hock. The hock is the actual joint – not the upright bone so erroneously described as the hock.

The muscle is extremely important in the hindquarters. There must be no hint of flabbiness in the leg and the dog should be capable of running long distances and indulging in a powerful sprint.

It is significant that a great many of our 'jumpers' who find escaping so easy have a comparatively straight stifle; they are also excellent movers.

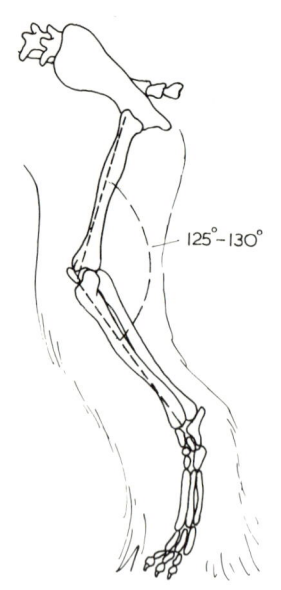

The angle of the stifle joint

The legs must be set square on the body with the feet coming down straight and firm. They should never slope in together on the lower bone causing 'knocking hocks' or 'cow hocks'. Nor should there be any appearance of bowing on the femur and stifle.

Feet
A most important part of the dog, since they provide his base and stability. They must be well down on the ground but the Afghan must not be flatfooted. They are essentially a large, long foot and the toes should not be flattened and splayed out. Nor should the front feet be up on the toes causing a terrier-type foot. The toes must be springy and well arched. On the hindfoot the whole appearance is longer and narrower and the pads must not be visible on either hind- or forefeet. The pasterns must be long and sloping and springy. The dog with a straight upright pastern has a much more stilted action which jars right up to the shoulder blade. It is significant to note that the whole of the front assembly balances together and the dog with a straight or upright shoulder usually has an equally upright pastern.

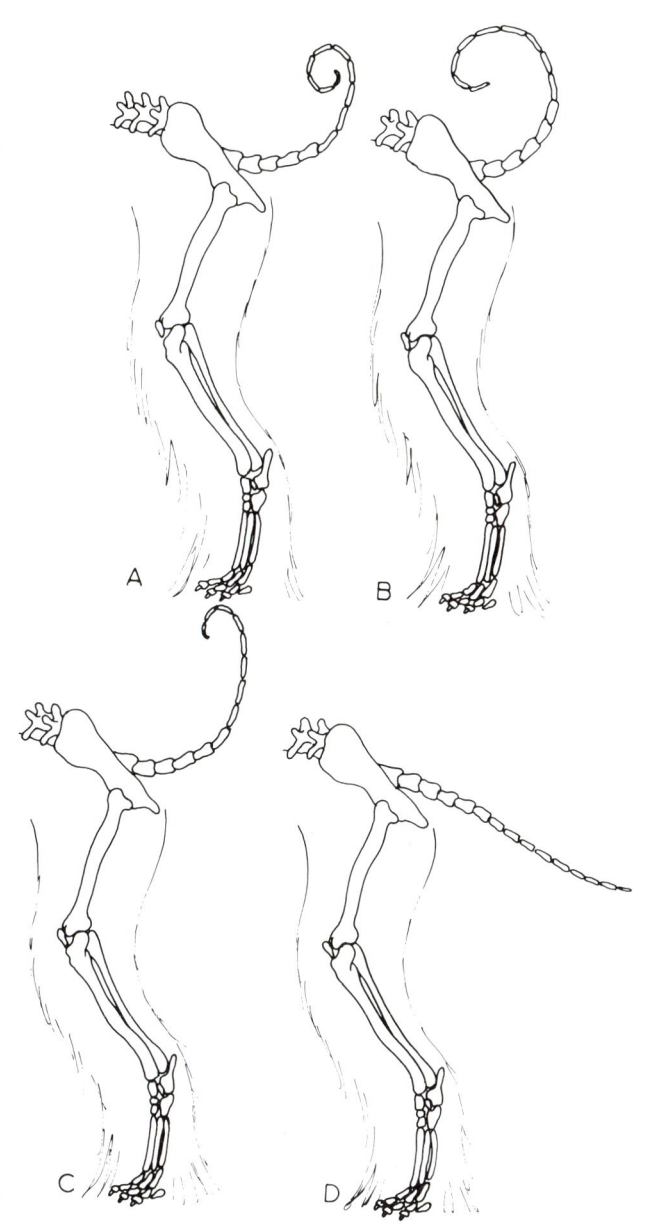

Tail sets: **A** is correctly placed; **B** has a teapot handle; **C** is too high set; **D** has an awkward angle and no ring

Tail

Once more the length is not specified but is left to the imagination. The ring should not be too close to the rump when the tail is raised but should be at a distance, giving sufficient length to balance the whole dog. A general rule of thumb could state that the tip of the tail, unrolled, should ideally reach the hock. When the dog is standing the tail is relaxed and can be lowered but should not resemble limp string dangling behind. It should be raised in action but since it is an extension of the backbone it should emerge at an easy angle, not an awkward, upright stilted one, and though carried gaily it should never be carried over the back. There should be a ring at the end to give the characteristic doughnut impression, but the very loose ring that is beginning to creep into the breed does not give such a typical appearance. A bushy, overfeathered squirrel tail is not acceptable.

Coat

The characteristic glamour feature of the Afghan! It is the coat pattern which contributes largely to type in the Afghan hound with the attractive saddle of shorter darker hair along the back. In the Afghans that come from Afghanistan the saddle is, even at an early age, quite pronounced and consists of hair of a very definite coarser texture. Unfortunately, in the breeding for longer coats and the constant competition for more and more flowing length, the characteristic saddle is rapidly disappearing and it is to be hoped that breeders of integrity will do their best to rectify this sad failing.

Although the hair on the foreface is short and smooth there is often in puppies a soft distinctive fluffy growth which can be either sparse or very thick, and which can, in some cases, practically obscure the whole of the foreface. This is perfectly correct and does not need removing. Indeed a great deal of the charm of the young puppy comes from the whiskered monkey face with the bright little eyes peering through a fuzz of puppy whiskers.

The bare pasterns which used to be quite common have now virtually disappeared. When they are seen, however, it must be remembered that they are perfectly correct and should not on any account be faulted. They often occur with a rather more

At four months puppies are easily recognisable as Afghans even without the distinctive coats (*Chris Hill*)

sparsely covered foot which instead of being completely and heavily furred over has tufts of hair growing from between the toes. This has a tendency to make the foot look smaller but if it is compared with the ones hidden under hairy 'overshoes' it will be seen that in fact the foot is equally up to size. The silky top-knot gets longer and longer; at one time it sprang from the forehead in a most regal widow's peak and formed a proud crest of long silky hair growing backwards on top of the head enhancing the proud fierce appearance of the 'king of the dogs' and my own feeling is that the curtains which now hang heavily on each side of the forehead have not added positively to the character of the Afghan expression.

The coat must not be interfered with in any way. If it is kept decently groomed it will grow into a natural pleasing shape and there is absolutely no need to use scissors to 'improve' the outline, or to cut away neck coat. Saddles can be tidied up if the edges are wispy.

On the whole this constant breeding for coat is losing us type with the disappearance of the saddle and the immense layers of coat which completely hide both form and outline of the dog and which tend to confuse the free-striding appearance by 'flipping' when the dog moves. Muscle tone is also being sacrificed for the preservation of the coat since these dogs are not allowed to run free amongst the trees and long grass in case of tearing or matting.

Colours
All colours are acceptable but it is not desirable to have white markings on the nose in the case of a dog which will be shown.

Size
Afghans show considerable variation of up to 5cm in the height to the shoulder where the measurement is taken. Many dogs are over the standard and in a well proportioned and balanced hound this is not always immediately noticeable, but a dog below the standard is clearly obvious. There is the dangerous tendency for a small dog to look feminine and a large, heavily built dog has a tendency to appear cloddy. Similarly a bitch that is too large can easily lose her

femininity and nothing looks worse than a doggy bitch.

Faults
These are often very obvious but no dog should be instantly penalised because of one clear fault. It should be taken into account with his virtues, always remembering that no dog is faultless. Also remember, when breeding, that faults will be handed down from generation to generation and therefore the closer that one can breed to the standard the better.

Entirety
The lack of a testicle must be considered as a fault and is definitely hereditary; monorchids are fertile and capable of breeding and will at the same time be reproducing their own fault. Nevertheless it is no longer, in the show ring, a matter for immediate dismissal, although at one time they were not allowed at all. The condition must be considered as one fault amongst others, although the seriousness of its acceptance or not will depend entirely on the attitude of the judge.

Hopefully the standard will be retained and, equally hopefully, breeding purely for glamour in the show ring will end and we shall see, not mere glamour dogs, but the proud, strong, active and incomparable Afghan hound.

Appendices

APPENDIX 1 UK AFGHAN CLUBS

Afghan Hound Association—Mrs A. Adams, Cockle Point, Marine Walk, Hayling Island, Hants PO11 9PQ

Afghan Hound Club of Wales—Mrs H. Bruton, 1 Penylan Place, Cardiff

Afghan Hound Society of Northern Ireland—Mr D. Burke, 38 Beehill Park North, Saintfield Road, Belfast BT8 4NZ

Afghan Hound Society of Scotland—Mrs I. Gibbon, 40 Chapel Place, Inverkeithing, Fife

East of England Afghan Club—Mrs D. Bowdler-Townsend, Old Park Farmhouse, Gunby, Spilsby, Lincs

Midland Afghan Hound Club—Mr T. L. Ashworth, 38 Northampton Road, Market Harborough, Leicester LE16 9HE

North-Eastern Afghan Hound Society—Miss M. Hardy, Burnmoor Farmhouse, Golf Course Road, Houghton-le-Spring, Co Durham

Northern Afghan Hound Society—Mrs J. Chilton, 21 Saville Road, Gatley, Cheshire SK8 4BY

Southern Afghan Club—Mrs D. M. Gie, West Down, Hastlingleigh, Ashford, Kent

Western Afghan Hound Club—Mrs C. A. Hill, 3 The Nydon, Catcott, Nr Bridgwater, Somerset

APPENDIX 2 US AFGHAN CLUBS

Afghan Hound Club of Greater Phoenix—Mona Denton, 1202 E Gardenia Drive, Phoenix, Arizona 95020

Afghan Hound Club of California—Mrs B. J. Morgan, PO Box 1357, Burbank, Calif 91507

Northern California Afghan Hound Club—Mrs Joanne Montesano, 4757 Rollinghills Way, Castro Valley, Calif 94546

Afghan Hound Club of Greater Denver—Mrs Daphane Lowe, 7459 E Easter Drive, Englewood, Colorado 80110

Afghan Hound Club of South Florida—Mrs Thene Castle, 4311 Northwest 9 Court, Coconut Creek, Florida 33066

Tara Afghan Hound Club—Miss Sheila McCrimmon, 2758 Five Forks Rd (Route 3), Lawrenceville, Ga 30245

Afghan Hound Club of Hawaii—Lynne Richardson, 46–324 Haiku Road No 109, Kaneohe, Hawaii 96744

Afghan Hound Club of Greater Chicago—Miss Cheryl Checker, 15 W 754 72nd Street, Hinsdale, Ill 60521

New Orleans Afghan Hound Club—Jim Vining, 733 Carrollwood Dr, Apt 68, Gretna, Louisiana

Potomac Afghan Hound Club (Washington, DC area)—Mrs Eleanor Creech, Box 12, Shady Side, Md 20867

Colonial Afghan Hound Club—Mrs Donna Conklin, Bolton Road, Harvard, Mass 01451

Afghan Hound Club of Greater Detroit—Mrs Karen Kasprzk, 12682 Riad, Detroit, Michigan

Greater Twin Cities Afghan Hound Club—Jane Conolly, 1572 Hastings Ave, Newport, Minn 55055

Afghan Hound Club of St Louis—Mrs Nancy Kantor, 7423 Shaftesbury, St Louis, Mo 63130

Afghan Hound Club of Omaha—Mrs Karen Murphy, 5345 N 60th Street, Omaha, Nebraska 68104

Afghan Hound Club of Northern New Jersey—Mr Michael Canalizo, 30 E Woodbine Drive, Freeport, NY 11520

Afghan Hound Assn of Long Island—Mrs Helen Ferrara, 27 Selden Blvd, Centereach, NY 11720

Finger Lakes Afghan Hound Club—Mrs Yvonne Fish, 33 Trowbridge Tr, Pittsford, NY 14534

Afghan Hound Club of Southwestern Ohio—Ms Carol Muccino, 1787 Wanninger, Cincinnati, Ohio 45230

APPENDIX 2 US AFGHAN CLUBS

Midwest Afghan Hound Club—Mr Fred Stock, 1508 Hunter Road, Verona, Pa 15147

Delaware Valley Afghan Hound Club—Janet Astroth Carr, RD 1, Box 175A, Lincoln University, Pa 19352

Afghan Hound Club of Austin—Lynda Robyn, PO Box 4894, Austin, Texas 78767

Afghan Hound Club of Dallas—Mrs Eugene Risedorph, 3409 Doty Lane, Arlington, Texas 76016

Afghan Hound Club of Greater Houston—Mrs Johanna Tanner, 1207 Crawford, Friendswood, Texas 77546

Richmond Afghan Hound Club—Mrs Michael McMunn, 2707 Stuart Avenue, Richmond, Va 23220

Evergreen Afghan Hound Club—Sandi Holden, 279 Lake Desire Drive N, Renton, Washington 98055

Afghan Hound Club of Greater Milwaukee—Mrs Joanne Daley, 508 N 114th St, Wauwatosa, Wisconsin

Bibliography

Macdonald-Brierley, Joan. *This is The Afghan* (T. F. H. Publications, 1965)
Crump, M. *The Helping Hand* (J. Cartledge, Ruislip, 1967)
Page-Elliot, Rachel. *Dog Steps* (Howell Book House, 1973)
Frankling, Eleanor. *Dog Breeding and Genetics* (Popular Dogs, 1961)
Harrison, Charles. *The Afghan Hound* (Popular Dogs, 1971)
Horner, Tom. *Take Them Round Please* (David & Charles, 1974)
Hutchinson's Dog Encyclopaedia (1934)
The Kennel Club Standards (Sporting Breeds) (The Kennel Club)
McDowell, Lyon, Howell. *The Dog In Action* (Bailey Bros. & Swinfen, 1950)
Miller, Constance, & Gilbert, Edward. *The Complete Afghan Hound* (Howell Book House, 1965)
Smythe, R. H., MRCVS. *The Anatomy of Dog Breeding* (Popular Dogs, 1962)
The Conformation of The Dog (Popular Dogs, 1957)
Schneck, Stephen with Norris, Nigel, BVSc, MRCVS.
Collins A To Z of Dog Care (Collins, 1975)
Our Afghans (Weddell Publications, America, monthly)

Acknowledgements

I am most grateful for the help that I have received from so many people in the preparation of this book and I would particularly like to thank the following: Mr Ronald Adams for his help with photographs and Mrs Ann Adams for supplying me with information from the Afghan Hound Association; Mr Charles Harrisson and Mr Nigel Harcourt-Brown MRCVS, BVSc, for checking sections of my manuscript; the Ministry of Agriculture, Fisheries and Food for information about exports; Mr Tom Horner for allowing me to quote from his book *Take Them Round Please*; *Dog World* for the use of Stafford Somerfield's article; Hutchinson Publishing Co. for permission to quote from *Hutchinson's Dog Encyclopaedia*; Mrs Sharon Jackson, of America, Miss Carla Molinari of Portugal, Mr Norman Huidobro of Spain, Herr Frankenburger of Germany, Mr and Mrs Tonks of Australia, Mrs June Bracey of S. Africa, and Mr R. Margrain of Ireland for their information about the breed and overseas showing; Mr Ali Hupka for his help with pictures; Mr Len Hitch for information about the Rescue Service; Mr John Callow for information about Afghan racing; The Southern Afghan club for permission to quote from articles in the *Southern Afghan Review*; Connie Miller for permission to reproduce one of her articles; Ruth Weddell of Weddell Publications for permission to reprint from the magazine *Our Afghans*; Walter C. Chapman III for permission to reprint from articles in the magazine *Showcase*; Mr White for permission to Reproduce the Animal Health Trust Whelping Box; Mr and Mrs Peers Carter, and the late Mrs Marna Dods, for their information, advice and interest, and my husband for his help and encouragement.

Index

acquiring an Afghan, 13
Adams, Mr and Mrs R., 155
advertisements, 13
Afghan Hound Association, 175;
  ethics, 18, 83;
  racing, 180
Afghanistan, 144, 159
Afghan racing, 180
afterbirths, 90, 91;
  retention of, 92
after sales service, 15, 28
age:
  mating, 83, 95;
  old age, 70;
  of purchase, 18
Ajman kennel, 154
Akaba kennel, 160
Alyshan kennel, 157
Amps, Mrs, 146, 149, 150
Amudarya kennel, 156
anal glands, 62
ancestry, 79
Andrews, Mrs Ann, 159
angulation:
  shoulder, 189;
  hindquarters, 191
Animal Health Trust, 88
appearance, 183, 186
Arkenstone kennel, 173
Atkins, Mrs Ivy, 159
Australian National Kennel Council, 164
Avidin, 104
awards, 119, 131, 139, 140

Badakshan kennel, 155
Balkh, 144
Baluch hounds, 145
Baraclai Levy, J. de, 47, 152
Barakzai kennel, 155
Barbille kennel, 155
Barff, Captain, 149
Baria, Maharaja of, 88

Barnes, Miss Helen, 156
Barnett, Dr Keith, 79
Baruchzy hounds, 145
bathing, 54, 115
Beare, Mr and Mrs, 174
Bell Murray, Major and Mrs, 149, 151
Bell Murray type, 148, 151
biscuit, 45
Biotin, 104
bitch:
  in season, 82;
  in whelp, 84, 89;
  loan of, 81
  newly whelped, 92, 93
Bletchingley kennel, 152, 165, 166, 168
Boardman, Mrs Lois, 160
body: 190;
  building, 47;
  proportion, 20
Bondor kennel, 156
bone flour, steamed, 99, 100, 104
Booth, Miss Monica, 159
Borst, Mrs Thelma, 174
Bowler-Townsend, Mrs Diana, 155
Bracey, Mrs J, 166
Branwen kennel, 154
breeders, 13, 15
breeding: 75;
  exaggeration for showing, 79;
  in breeding, 79;
  line breeding, 79
breed clubs, 175;
  magazines, 181
breeding kennels, 13
breed standard, 20, 123, 175
Brooks, Alan, 156
bugs, 57

caesarian birth, 91
Calahorra kennel, 164
calcium deficiency, 68
Callow, John, 180
Camri kennel, 162

INDEX

care and management, 45
Carloway kennel, 152, 153, 159, 164
Carter, Mr and Mrs Peers, 148, 150, 159
Cathcart kennel, 166
challenge certificate, 131, 140
Chaman, 145
Chaman kennel, 151, 163
Chandharah kennel, 164
Chandigarh kennel, 170
characteristics, 185
choosing a puppy, 17
Clark, Mr and Mrs B., 158
Coastwind kennel, 162, 164
coat, 185, 194
cod liver oil, 104
collars, 38
colour, 26, 185, 196
commercial foods, 107
Complete Afghan Hound, 162
conditions (breeding and sale), 81
Couper, Mrs, 151
coupling, 191
Cove kennel, 151
cow hocks, 21, 192
critiques, 139
Cross, Fred, 124
croup, 190
Crown Crest kennel, 160, 164
culling, 95
cut paws, 65

Dally, Lyle, 164
Davlen kennel, 156
deknotting, 54
Denham, Michael, 162
dentition, 22
destructiveness, 35
Devitt-Gilleney, Mrs Sheila, 153
dew claws, 64
diarrhoea, 62
di-calcium phosphate, 68, 99, 104
Dicmar kennel, 162
Diet:
 in old age, 71;
 in-whelp bitch, 85;
 newly-whelped bitch, 93;
 nursing bitch, 99;
 puppy, 103, 104, 105;
 older puppy, 105;
 weaning, 102, 103
dish face, 22
Dods, Mrs Marna, 153
Dog World, 16, 119, 125
Doody, Marjorie and Colette, 174
Dove, Miss Jennifer, 157
drinking water, 49
Drinkwater, Mrs E., 151
Dyke, Mrs Isobel, 159

ears, 17, 22, 54, 116
ear fringes, 116
eczema, 67
Edmonds, John, 156
El Kairas kennel, 168
El Kamas kennel, 87, 168
Enriallac kennel, 172
enteritis, 62
entropion, 62
Etheridge, Mrs Barbara, 155
Ethics:
 breeders, 18, 78, 83, 95;
 judging, 128, 129
euthanasia, 72
exercise, 49
exporters, 98
exporting, 97
export pedigree, 98
extractions, 64
eyes, 17, 61, 183, 187

fallaway, 190
false pregnancies, 65
fat-free diet, 68
fattening up, 47
faults, 185, 197
feeding, 45, 47
feeding habits, 33, 34
feet, 25, 184, 192
Finch, Mrs Kay, 160
fish, 49
flaked maize, 46
fleas, 57
Floyd, Reg, 152
foot care, 64
Ford, Rev David, 155
forelegs, 18
Fosse, Mdme, 160, 170
foster mothers, 93
fractures, 67
Frankenburger, Herr and Fr, 168
fronts, 21
Furbari kennel, 164
Furber, Mrs Helen, 164

Gainsborough, Mr and Mrs, 166
garlic, 47
Garrymhor kennel, 151
gestation, 40
Geufron kennel, 78
Ghazni, 77
Gibbs, Sqn Ldr and Mrs, 82
Gilbert, Edward, 84
Grandeur kennel, 84
green star, 89
grooming, 22
growing puppy diet, 52
growth, 50

205

INDEX

Hall, Bill, 155
Hampton, Mr and Mrs, 163
hand rearing, 93
Harcourt-Brown family, 159
Harris, Paul and Carol, 156, 171
Harrisson, Mr and Mrs Charles, 154
Harrison, Mrs R. Y., 152
head, 21, 183, 187
health certificate, 98
heart worms, 60
hereditary conditions, 69
hernias, 67
hindlegs, 25
hindquarters, 184, 191
hip bones, 24
hip dysplasia, 69
Hitch, Len, 178
hocks, cow, 21, 192
Holloway, Mr and Mrs, 163
Horner, Tom, 123, 124
Horningsea kennel, 153, 165
house training, 30
Hughes, Mrs Ruth, 155
Hullabaloo kennel, 162
Hunt-Crowley, Miss S., 164
Hupka, Ali, 155
Hutchinson's Dog Encyclopaedia, 145

Ide, Mrs, 152
identity, 36
identification, 101, 102
in-breeding, 79
induced whelping, 91
inoculation, 16, 59
in-season bitch, 82
insurance, 26, 181
in-whelp bitch: 84;
  diet for, 85
Irish champions, 173

Jackson, Monroe and Sharon, 162
Jagai kennel, 165, 168
Jalalabad kennel, 152
James, Mrs, 166
judging: 121;
  courage, 124;
  ethics, 128, 129;
  pattern, 137;
  procedure, 136, 139;
  qualifications, 177;
  reports, 139;
  training schemes, 129, 177
judging book, 136

Kabul, El, kennel, 151
Kairas, El, kennel, 168
Kalbikhan kennel, 155
Kamas, El, kennel, 168
Kandahar, El, kennel, 166

Katwiga kennel, 168, 169
Kean, Miss Patricia, 69, 154
Kennedy, Dr Gerda, 163
Kelly, Bill, 172
Kennels (breeding), 13
Kennel Club, 15, 119, 125
  rules, 131, 139
Khanabad kennel, 154
Kharrissar kennels, 159
Khinjan kennel, 156, 164
Khorrassan kennel, 153
Knight, Miss Gillian, 155
knots, 54
knowledge of the standard, 12
Koh-i-Noor kennel, 159
Koolaba kennel, 157
Kophi kennel, 163

Larade kennel, 163
leads, 38
lead training, 37, 38
leaving alone, 42
lice, 57
line breeding, 79
living quarters, 33, 35
loan of bitch, 81
lying down, 37

Madigan, Mrs Cynthia, 154, 170
magazines:
  Our Afghans, 10;
  Showcase, 93, 181;
  Southern Afghan Club, 181
Maharajah of Baria, 170
mammary tumours, 66
mange, 66
Manson, Mrs Jean, 151, 172
Marchonique kennel, 163
Matchett, Mrs, 163
maternity kit, 86
Mathers, Mrs Ann, 173
mating: 82, 83;
  age of, 83, 95;
  time of, 97
Margrain, Robert, 173
Marsh, Dr and Mrs, 163
Matthews, Miss Marjorie, 152
Mazar-i-Sharif kennel, 168
McCarthy, Denis, 156
McKenzie, Miss Elizabeth, 69, 154
McKenzie, Major, 144
meat, 46, 48
Metewand kennel, 173
milk, 49
milk fever, 93
Miller, Constance, 10, 162
Ministry of Agriculture, 98
Mirsamir kennel, 159
misconceptions, 10

INDEX

Miyasht kennel, 159, 165
Molinari, Miss Carla, 172
Moonswift kennel, 86, 89, 155, 165, 174
monorchidism, 197
Montravia kennel, 156
Morris, Mrs, 166
Morton, Mrs Ida, 152
mouth, 184, 188
movement, 21
Myria, El, kennel, 163

name, 36
narrow front, 21
neck, 24, 188
Netheroyd kennels, 152
nettles, 46
newly-whelped bitch:
 cleaning, 92;
 diet, 93
Nilbud kennels, 174
Northern Afghan Hound Asscn., 152
North, Miss Gloria, 154
nursing bitch, 100

oats, 46
obesity, 48
occiput, 22
old age and parting, 70
older puppy diet, 106
Orange Manege, Van de, kennel, 166, 168
Our Afghans, 10
Our Dogs, 16, 114
outcross, 80
outdoor training, 40

Pandjah kennels, 170
pancreatic deficiency, 168
parades of champions, 177
pasterns, 184
pattern-judging, 136, 137
Paton, Mrs Anna, 156
Patrols kennel, 152
Paulchen, Graham, 164
Pauptit, M Eta, 168
Pede, Lt Col Wallace, 163
pedigree, 78, 83;
 export, 98
pink haws, 17, 61
Pollock, Mr and Mrs Sydney, 155
Pooghan kennel, 156
Porter, Dr Betsy, 151, 160
preparation for showing, 115, 116
procedure for:
 judging, 135;
 showing, 118
progressive retinal atrophy, 70
proportions, 21, 22

punishment, 32
puppies:
 abnormal, 92;
 appearance, 18, 21;
 diet, 105;
 grooming, 37;
 whiskers, 22, 194
puppy classes, 109
purchasing a puppy, 13-29
Pushtikuh kennel, 151, 152, 164

qualifications for judging, 130
Queensway kennel, 163

Race, Mrs Clair, 155
racing, 180
registrations, 84
Reklaw kennel, 166
rescue dogs and schemes, 178
retained afterbirth, 90, 92
ribs, 184, 190
rickets, 68
Rifka's kennel, 155
Rigouleaux, M, 170
Riley, Mrs Peggy, 152
Roche, David, 153, 164
Rodde, Mrs Erica, 168
Roman nose, 187
Rosados, Antonio, 172
roundworms, 59
Runmarker, Birgitha, 168

Sacheverell kennel, 159
saddle, 185, 194
Sams, Mrs Dawn, 156
Saringas kennel, 157
Scheherezade kennel, 152, 163
Schelling, Mrs Lynette, 164
Schultz, Mrs, 170
seasons, 82
seaweed powder, 47
sedatives, 116
Semple, Miss Helen, 152
Shaaltarah kennel, 164
Shangrila kennel, 163
Shanshu kennel, 158, 165
Sharpe, Mrs Molly, 151, 160, 172
Shay, Mrs Sunny, 162
Sherdil kennel, 172
Shirekhan kennel, 166
shoulder angulation, 24, 189
Showcase, 181
show puppy, 21
size, 185, 196
Skilton, Mrs Barbara, 164
skin troubles, 67
skull, 22, 183, 187
Slatyer, Stuart and Wendy, 164
sleeping quarters, 35, 57

207

INDEX

showing: 109;
  classification, 114;
  equipment, 116;
  preparation, 115;
  procedure, 117;
  training, 111, 112
Snelling, Miss Eileen, 153
snoods, 55, 56, 116
social training, 30-7
Somerfield, Stafford, 125
Southern Afghan Club, 177, 179, 181
Souza, Richard, 162
spaying, 66
standard, 20, 123, 182
steamed bone flour, 104
stewarding, 135, 136
Stites, Earl and Betty, 162, 181
Stoll, Dick and Marcia, 162
stop, 183, 187
Stormhill kennel, 160
stud dogs: 79, 83;
  fees, 80
Summerwine kennel, 162
supplements, 104
Swallow, Eric, 156

Taff kennel, 166
tail, 24, 184, 194
Tait, Eric, 166
Tajmahal kennel, 166
Takabbor kennel, 155
Take them round, please, 123, 124
taking temperatures, 69
talcum powder, 50
tape worms, 59
Tarril kennel, 155
Taylor, Mrs Barbara, 157
teeth, 63
temperature, 69
thyroid gland, 48
Tiohi-Tikan kennel, 168
toes, 192
tooth extraction, 64
tourniquet, 65

training: 30;
  car journeys, 43;
  lead, 38;
  sit and down, 37;
  to be left alone, 42;
  showing, 111, 112, 114
training classes, 114
training judges, 129, 130, 177
tranquillizers, 35
Trolle, Ingrid af, 166
tube feeding, 94
tumours, 66
Turkuman kennel, 152

undershot mouth, 22

vaccines, 59, 60
Vale Negro kennel, 172
Van de Orange Manege kennel, 165, 168
Veldspringer kennel, 174
Venn, Miss Doris, 152
Vishnu kennel, 154
vitamin D, 31
vitamin supplements and conditioners, 53

Walkden-Sturgeon, 157
Walker, Mr, 166
weaning, 102-4
weight, 185
weight and growth chart, 101
Westmill kennel, 151
Westover kennel, 152
whelping: 89-92;
  accommodation, 42, 43, 86, 87, 88;
  cleaning bitch, 92;
  diet, 93
whelping box, 85, 88
Withington, Virginia and Sandy, 160
Wood, Mrs, 151
worming, 59, 108
worms, 59
wry mouth, 22, 188

yeast products, 104
yellow pages, 13, 14, 15